D0960834

It's possible for your pain to propel you to a place of wholeness rather than defeat. With humor and deep wisdom, Katherine and Jay share lessons that have been won through extreme hardship but that are universally applicable to anyone's story of pain. This book is worth every minute of your time.

TIM TEBOW, former NFL quarterback,
current professional baseball player,
and author of *Through My Eyes* and *Shaken*

The space between what you want and what you get is called "unmet expectations." Life didn't turn out like you'd hoped? It didn't for Katherine and Jay. Reading their story will help you understand yours. This is a profound and surprisingly happy book. Please read it.

MAX LUCADO, pastor and bestselling author
of *How Happiness Happens*

Trust the voices that have been tested. Because those who've been tested speak truth that can be trusted. Katherine and Jay Wolf have been tested, and they speak what is tried and true—and absolutely transformative. Hold this catalytic book gently—because once you read it, you will be forever changed. Because you aren't holding *ideas* about how to *endure* suffering—you are holding *igniting hope* that every single one of us needs: the tried, tested, true, and proven way through hard seasons, as told by brave survivors-thrivers who actually, daily, literally, *incarnate the truth* about how to *suffer strong*.

ANN VOSKAMP, *New York Times* bestselling author
of *The Broken Way* and *One Thousand Gifts*

Incredible people who together are a mighty force, Katherine and Jay have a special place in our hearts. Their story isn't what they thought life would be like, but they have been—as a family—a pillar of what it looks like to suffer strong. They inspire us every day to live and love and to walk and weep with the strength of God in our spine. As you take the next steps in learning how to suffer strong, you will see God refine broken pieces in your life and unlock power like you have never experienced before. This broken piece is your microphone for all that God wants to do in you and through you, and we believe it will be beautiful.

LEVI AND JENNIE LUSKO, lead pastors
of Fresh Life Church

There is a powerful credibility found in the words of this remarkable couple as they point us to the One they've grown to know through the fire. With humor and honesty, Katherine and Jay each use their unique voice to help us reconcile what we all wrestle with in this life—God's goodness and human suffering. *Suffer Strong* will make you laugh and think, and it'll hopefully leave you more equipped to see how God so sovereignly redeems our suffering.

MAYA MOORE, four-time WNBA champion,
two-time Olympic gold medalist, and advocate
for redeeming our criminal justice system

SUFFER STRONG

SUFFER STRONG

How to Survive Anything by
Redefining Everything

KATHERINE & JAY WOLF

ZONDERVAN

Suffer Strong
Copyright © 2020 by Katherine Wolf and Jay Wolf

Requests for information should be addressed to:
Zondervan, *3900 Sparks Dr. SE, Grand Rapids, Michigan 49546*

Zondervan titles may be purchased in bulk for educational, business, fundraising, or promotional use. For information, please email SpecialMarkets@Zondervan.com.

ISBN 978-0-310-34457-5 (hardcover)

ISBN 978-0-310-35819-0 (audio)

ISBN 978-0-310-34459-9 (ebook)

The authors are represented by the literary agency of Alive Literary Agency, www.aliveliterary.com.

Cover design: Curt Diepenhorst
Cover photo: Cameron Powell
Interior design: Kait Lamphere

Printed in the United States of America

19 20 21 22 23 24 25 26 27 28 29 /LSC/ 13 12 11 10 9 8 7 6 5 4 3 2 1

For all the broken bodies, broken
brains, and broken hearts . . .
there is MORE.

CONTENTS

FOREWORD

Have you ever met people you knew would change your whole life? When we sat on stage with Katherine and Jay for the first time at Passion 2017, that's the sense we had. We believed a seismic shift was about to happen—not just for that moment, in the lives of the fifty thousand people who surrounded the platform, but *through* that moment as a generation was going to be changed. And that's exactly what happened.

It wasn't the first time Katherine and Jay had been at a Passion gathering. Several years before, at Passion 2013, their lives had been greatly impacted by the reality that their suffering could and would be used for God's glory. They were experiencing a glorious rebirth rooted in the staggering reality that there was purpose in their pain. Now, four years later, they were speaking at the same event in the very same stadium, powerfully sharing their journey through suffering and loss—not as victims, but as those who were overcoming through the power of God.

We have met few people like our friends Katherine and Jay. In spite of their circumstances, they continue to defiantly choose joy. Katherine is one of the most positive, hopeful, and encouraging people on the planet. Not to mention, she is tough! Who else has had a brain stem stroke that left them partially paralyzed and in a wheelchair, and yet still insists on standing when they pray at church? And who can fully describe the servant-hearted kindness and leadership of Jay Wolf? On their own, they are magnificent, but together, they are a mighty force for the kingdom of God.

We believe God is using Katherine and Jay in extraordinary ways to reshape the lens through which people view their suffering and pain. They are disrupting the deep lie that a pain-free life is the only life where there is joy, flipping the view that God only works and brings about good where there is an absence of hardship and suffering.

We see in Scripture that God has a track record of taking the way things are and turning them upside down. From the very start of creation, God took what was formless and empty and spoke light into the darkness. In an instant, He set a precedent that would weave throughout Scripture: that with God, not only is transformation possible, but it is also His purpose. Weakness becomes strength. Defeat becomes victory. Death becomes life. He is the God of redemption, and He does this in the granular and the great, in the details of our lives, and in the eternal destiny of our souls. Jesus changes everything.

But like Katherine and Jay's story, we don't always have control over our circumstances. We can't always plan for every outcome or situation. But that doesn't make us helpless. Even though we may be victims of a fallen world, we can be victors in Christ. We have been given the power to overcome any trial or tribulation. This is what it means when we read 2 Corinthians 4:8–9: "We are hard pressed on every side, but not crushed; perplexed, but not in despair; persecuted, but not abandoned; struck down, but not destroyed." Only seven verses later, Paul writes these words: "Therefore we do not lose heart."

Paul echoes back what Jesus told the disciples in John 16:33: "In this world you will have trouble. But take heart! I have overcome the world." This is Katherine and Jay's story—in this world they have had troubles. We can all say amen to having troubles. But here is what makes their story so powerful: suffering is not something we have to avoid. It is not the end of the story. In fact, as Katherine often says, it is the beginning.

This is what *Suffer Strong* is about. Every chapter focuses on redefining our stories by the grace of Jesus. The result is new hope, new strength, and a new foundation that will stand firm in all circumstances of life.

Katherine and Jay Wolf are such beautiful carriers of this message, and we are convinced that *Suffer Strong* truly has the potential to change everything. Katherine and Jay aren't sharing from their perfection, but from their transformed weakness. They have experienced the richness and reward of hard-fought battles. They have come through to the other side scarred, but standing, wounded, but victorious. And though the landscape of their lives has been significantly altered, God's purpose for their lives remains. His plans for them are as sure today as they were the second before Katherine's near-fatal stroke. Because of this, every page of *Suffer Strong* echoes the faithfulness of God.

We believe that God intentionally puts people in our paths who will cause an immediate and tangible impact, shifting the trajectories of our lives forever. Katherine and Jay have been those people for us, and we believe God has raised them up to be two of the most significant voices to His people. For too long, the church has left in the dust those with seeming unanswered "miracle prayers" and residual disabilities, leaving them to feel as though they fell short in their faith and now must accept diminished dreams in God's purposes and plans. Katherine and Jay offer the opposite view as they live out of the confidence that because of their disability, not in spite of it, God is advancing His will and bringing great glory to His name.

We are ecstatic that after a cross-country move, Katherine and Jay now call Passion City Church their home church. It is one of the greatest honors in this season to watch from up close as God continues to confirm in their marriage and family the truth of 1 Thessalonians 5:24: "The one who calls you is faithful, and he will do it."

If you haven't met them yet, you're going to fall in love with our friends as their beauty, humor, and honesty drip from every page. As they lead you, we believe what you once saw as pain can become your treasured platform. Your suffering in this present time may actually turn into your greatest point of access to a broken and desperate world.

Katherine and Jay are testaments to this truth, boldly choosing to view their suffering as "light and momentary troubles" that are gaining for them "an eternal glory that far outweighs" every trial and tribulation (2 Corinthians 4:17). They are learning to *suffer strong*, and we could not be more honored to walk alongside them in their journey.

Turn the page and get ready to step into a brand-new way of life.

Louie and Shelley Giglio, pastor, Passion City Church,
and cofounders of the Passion Movement

HOPE PREVAILS

Jay

Our stories are glorious. They're also painful, unfair, scary, and almost always quite different from what we thought they would be. Yet it seems that those parts might be the very means through which the glory is most revealed.

More than a decade ago, on an ordinary day, life as we knew it changed for Katherine and me in a matter of minutes. At the age of twenty-six, Katherine suffered a catastrophic brainstem stroke that robbed her of her ability to walk, talk, and even eat. She couldn't live in our home or be the mother she longed to be to our six-month-old son. And in the aftermath of our devastation, I was thrust into brand-new roles I never imagined I'd sign up for. I was still Katherine's husband, yes, but I was also caregiver and health care advocate. Every golden dream we'd anticipated just ahead on our journey—new baby, new career, new season, new hope upon hope for the life we thought we would have—was left hanging by the finest thread.

In our first book, *Hope Heals*, we shared our story of overwhelming loss and overcoming love that followed this life-altering event. In *Suffer Strong*, we trace the evolution from the story of what happened to us to the lessons we've learned along the way and the treasures we've found in the darkness. Profound suffering at a young age may seem like a tragedy—so much potential, so many dreams, all swept away in a moment. But as we've marinated in our experiences and shared them over these subsequent years, we've seen that our story is a microcosm of a much bigger one, a story being told through each of our lives—one of broken things being healed and nearly dead things springing forth into new life. This is ultimately the story of God in the world—holding it, healing it, hoping for it.

Human suffering takes so many forms, and it can be tempting to rank what's worthy of being deemed "real" suffering. But aren't we all struggling to live with realities we would not choose? Suffering in its simplest form comes in the space between what we thought would be and what is. That tension can rock us to our core, whether it's losing a job or facing a tough medical diagnosis, experiencing a bad breakup or managing a financial challenge, suffering depression or losing a loved one. Our humanity places each of us on this spectrum of pains, and the great irony is that we often isolate ourselves by saying, "My pain is so big, *no one* understands," or conversely, "My pain is so insignificant, *no one* would care."

The truth is, the experiences that feel most personal—like *no one else* could get it—are the most universal experiences in life. In the midst of our own pain and loss, Katherine and I have learned that suffering is suffering, and in every case it's possible to suffer strong. Life *defines* us, but suffering *redefines* us. Ultimately, hope *refines* us, transforming us from within in ways we never could have imagined.

Everyone is defined by a unique combination of things. When we come into this world, our identity is defined by things we didn't choose and can't alter—our families, our genetics, our personalities. We are further defined by our fears, wounds, and longings as we travel our individual paths. All of these components begin to form the unique parameters of who we are, the shape of our hearts, and the route to our future.

But as we live in the world, as we suffer and grow, we experience things that bump against the boundaries of what has defined us thus far, that chip away at and redefine our borders, and that sometimes shatter the life we've known. The real work, the hardest work, is to pick up the pieces and decide how to put them back together again. The new thing that emerges may not work the way it used to, but it can bend and stretch and change us in ways we come to treasure even more. As much as we recoil from suffering, it has the potential to show us who we are and who God is in ways that dramatically alter the way we live our lives. We can gain precious wisdom and deeper appreciation for the lives we've been given as we learn to suffer well—not as victims, but as overcomers.

We assume you're holding this book because you've been through some things—maybe some really, really hard things. For that, we are so sorry. But each of us has the opportunity to thrive in situations we never dreamed we'd have to experience.

As is often said, life's circumstances are out of our control, but our response to them is not. While suffering strong can be disorienting and painful at first, it's a journey that promises greater purpose, hope, and joy.

This book is the record of the journey we've chosen to show up for every day since everything changed. The good news of our story, and your story, is that there is always more to it. Through the depths of our own pain, Katherine and I have had an experience with God and with each other that has radically changed the way we think and live. One defining moment ultimately led to a redefining of everything—our marriage, our faith, our purpose, our very lives. Both of us have gained a transformed perspective and a supernatural strength, not in spite of the suffering we've endured, but because of it.

The lessons, struggles, strength, and hope we share in the pages ahead are ours, but they're yours too. They're for anyone willing to loosen their grip on what is precious to ultimately receive something even richer, deeper, and bigger. Suffering does not have to be the end of the story; rather, it can be the beginning of a new one. Let's tell each other that story together.

CHAPTER 1

INVISIBLE WHEELCHAIRS

Redefining Limitations

Katherine

I really hate clothes. I don't mean I prefer to go without them. And I actually do sort of care about what I wear in public—though cozy grandpa pajamas would be deemed socially appropriate to wear all the time if I ran the world. I just mean that I hate what clothes require. All the buying. All the trying on. All the laundering. All the hanging back up. All the swollen closets with nothing found in them to wear! I may have a little PTSD from my childhood spent in dressing rooms with certain unnamed family members who definitely did not hate clothes.

If that's your thing, then more power to you, but it has never brought me joy and usually just causes me unnecessary stress. Considering all the hard things I've been through and all the challenges I've overcome, I wonder, *Why the heck can't I get dressed easily? Why do I feel frozen? I'm a big girl! I should be able to put on my big girl panties and do something empowered like then put on my big girl shirt and pants.* But it never feels easy.

Sometimes life's daily struggles are harder to rally for than life's big struggles. We are all contradictions in this way, I suppose. And to be fair, our tiny 1920s California bungalow had closets big enough for doll clothes, so imagine me with my shaky balance and double vision standing on my tiptoes on a step stool to grab that perfect but just-out-of-reach accessory on the top shelf. I nearly died from a stroke; I won't die for fashion!

Imagine my delight when a few years ago I heard about a life-changing concept called a capsule wardrobe. Basically, it's a dozen or so different pieces of clothing all intended to go together. Grab some combo—ideally not three shirts; more like a combo that actually covers your whole body—and go! This kind of highly edited wardrobe takes some thinking through on the front end to select everything and pull it out, but it makes the day-to-day choosing so simple.

I've heard that many high-level CEOs employ a similar tactic. Humans can only make so many decisions in a day, so these businessmen and -women choose to wear pretty much the same thing all the time so they can save up all their good decision-making brainpower for things that actually matter a bit more. They are choosing to place limits on one area of their lives so that other areas can be more fully attended to.

I'm no CEO, but I'll take that idea and run with it! I still have a closet full of random clothes—I'm not great at purging either—but Jay helps me gather my limited capsule each week, and it's been surprisingly helpful. I'm no longer scared of my closet. If only the clothes later washed and hung themselves back up, I would be all in, but nothing's perfect.

Contrary to our most self-focused and consumeristic parts, we actually don't need constant access to every possible choice and every possible thing ever made in order to be satisfied. But the digital age has put the world's knowledge at our fingertips and presents an endless scroll of ideas in the palms of our hands. It tells us that all of it should be ours for the taking. How could less truly be more?

Everything in our culture and our minds pushes against this, though in reality, we can't even think through all our options, much less actually choose the best one. We're paralyzed by our abundance. More is more, and more is obviously too much! Our heads, like our closets, are overflowing with items we'll never need again, but we keep them around just in case. We never know when we might get invited to another Kentucky Derby–themed black-tie event! And it would certainly help if we thoroughly researched every hashtag related to #KentuckyDerby, #strangelybighats, #horses, #countryliving, #biscuits—you know how the trip down the virtual rabbit hole goes. So we keep the giant bedazzled hat for that one-day possibility and keep on scrolling, but in so doing we block our view of the things we actually need to be able to function, much less thrive, in our everyday lives.[1]

The idea of limiting our options as an avenue to flourishing isn't just good for business decisions or fashion choices. Some of the most brilliant creativity and useful clarity can result from con-straint. Flannery O'Connor writes, "Art transcends its limitations only by staying within them."[2] What first feels like a small and narrow focus eventually opens up a more expansive way of living. Yet we don't get to the fullness without first focusing inward.

Before I could eat again after my stroke, I'd strangely torture myself by watching reality TV cooking shows. It was a fantasy world through which I could vicariously enjoy food. And honestly, who doesn't love a good cooking show, especially one with the added drama of limiting the contestant to some painfully specific scenario or one totally random ingredient? Kimchi—let's do this! Squid ink it is! Sweetbreads are *what?* Now, let's get cooking, chefs! And these brilliant artists take the random item and make something interesting and totally new and hopefully even delicious out of it. Then we home chefs are inspired to embark on our own culinary journeys, gazing glassy-eyed into a strangely empty refrigerator, despite near-daily grocery store runs. Reality feels a little less inspiring. *I've got string cheese, ketchup, pickle juice, and a very old onion. Could this be an appetizer of some sort? What if I boil it?*

Flourishing within our limitations doesn't come quickly or easily; it takes much practice. But in time, redefining our constraints as opportunities rather than barriers helps expand our thinking in ways we never would have imagined otherwise. Limitations force us to look at what remains with more clarity too. They make us dig to the back of the fridge of our lives and find what we never knew we had and never knew we needed. And after finding it, we get to consider new and better ways to make it useful to us. When we mix all these parts of ourselves together—the neglected ones and the overstretched ones and the ones we never knew we had—we arrive at a place of not just surviving life but thriving in it.

Invisible Wheelchairs

You may wonder why a chapter on limitations written by a woman with disabilities has thus far discussed only clothing and food. Well, mainly because if I started talking about disabilities from the top, you may well have turned to the next chapter! And if you had, then you'd miss this big idea: we are *all* disabled. None of us have unlimited access to whatever we want or whatever we planned for our lives to look like. We are constrained by our marriages or our singleness, by our children or our childlessness, by our obligations or our debts, by obstacles real or imagined. No one enters life or leaves it without feeling bound by something. Some of us have physical wheelchairs, but we all have invisible wheelchairs inside us. None of us can do life all by ourselves. We need God, and we need each other.

Life with disabilities has been the most profoundly challenging and transformational experience of my life. It has given me a new perspective. It has invited me to lean into a different way of seeing God and living in the world. It has offered me a life of flourishing, not just in spite of my constraints, but because of them. In the Christian tradition of "the upside-down kingdom of God," the way to go up is to first be brought low. Over the years since the stroke, this paradoxical truth has been proven in my life.

Further, this life in a wheelchair has some strange perks, and it's not just getting to the front of the airport security line, though honestly, that's a big one. When Jay wheels me into a room, it's a fairly clear sign to anyone watching that this young-ish couple has been through a lot. All is not well. Whatever their story is, it's probably a hard one. The awareness triggered by seeing another person's physical disability can be a gift in terms of dismissing the automatic assumptions we tend to make when we see each other—assumptions that another's life must be easier and better than ours. For a moment, an obvious disability makes us think twice before judging a life and telling a story we actually don't know about another person.

Unless you're a sociopath or a troll on Twitter, you will likely look with compassion on us or folks like us with apparent outward disabilities. You'll stop and open the door or offer a courteous nod. You may ask, as nine out of ten children ask me, "What's wrong with your face?"—to which I say, "Nothing's wrong with it; my brain just got hurt, but I'm still smiling!" Conversely, you may avoid contact because you worry that I could have a communicable disease. You may yell down to me in loud, simple words as if I don't speak English. Or you may, like some pilots I've flown with, literally pin those little wings on my shirt—you know, the kind of wings young children are bribed with so they won't scream on the plane? Seriously, this has happened . . . twice. *Yes, that's so nice of you*, I think, *but the only motivation I need to not scream on this plane is one of those delightfully crispy cookies. Why don't you go grab me one of those!*

Physical disabilities are obvious and elicit a fairly typical response. But don't we all want other people around us to take one look at us and automatically know when we're not doing great? Maybe we should all get T-shirts printed that read, "Please treat me with care. I've been through a lot." Weirdly, some people still wouldn't wear them, particularly the ones who want us to think they have it all together. The problem is, those kinds of people are the most disabled of us all because they have no idea just how limited they actually are. Knowing you can't do everything is a harsh reality, but it's also a sweet gift. You couldn't do it all on your own anyway, and you don't have to.

Despite my attempt to universalize all our limitations as disabilities, I never want to downplay the uniquely painful realities of living in a physical world not made for one's physical body. It's very hard to empathize with the struggle and indignity of living with these kinds of disabilities until you've actually been in such a body or helped care for a loved one's. I've been hurt by strange stares and thoughtless questions. I've suffered the embarrassment of being forced to go in the back door of a restaurant, through the kitchen and past the trash bins, in order to squeeze into a dusty elevator full of boxes to get to the dinner table. I've had to make the walk of shame on multiple people's arms up the steps onto a stage that isn't wheelchair accessible at events at which I've been hired to speak. I've felt left out of my pre-stroke social life at times, knowing that it's just too much trouble for others to help me and accommodate me—and what's more, I wouldn't be able to hear people in the loud room or get around the crowded space anyway, so it's just better not to go at all.

Despite the struggles, I've got it *so easy* compared to most people with disabilities. I never take that for granted. This perspective has pulled me out of some deep pity parties. People with disabilities have the highest rates of depression, suicide, homelessness, divorce, and unemployment. Miraculously, that's not my story, but it breaks my heart that it's the story of so many others.

And as hard as it is to gain basic accessibility, even in the most developed countries like the United States, the circumstances for our brothers and sisters with disabilities in developing countries are so much more devastating. Often these friends live like lepers, completely isolated, shunned by their community, feeling cursed by God. Without simple tools like wheelchairs or function-saving surgeries, they may be homebound their entire lives or have to crawl and scrape their way across inaccessible and dangerous paths. There is little dignity for any of us persons with disabilities, which, by the way, is the largest minority group in the world according to the United Nations. And that makes our constraints feel very heavy and hardly an avenue to flourishing.

And yet when we think about the very able-bodied life of Jesus, we overlook the fact that, considering He was Almighty God, the physical world He came into was not made for Him either. He chose to constrain His God-ness to a very limited human body. He disabled Himself, so to speak. This incarnational theology offers something profound to folks with disabilities—and all of us, within our own constraints. Since Jesus willingly took on the constraints of humanity, then our own constraints can likewise be dignified. He chose to enter the mess and loss of living in our world. He chose to get low in order to ultimately be made high, so somehow we can too.

As if that wasn't inspiring enough, there's an even more breathtaking reality concerning our limitations than the dignity Jesus brings to them. The ultimate constraint on our lives is death. Yet in Jesus' death and resurrection, He draws an undeniably hopeful line in the sand and invites us to cross over it with Him. "Death did not defeat Me, so when you follow Me, you'll never have to be afraid that any of your constraints will ultimately defeat you either." Not only does this truth provide hope, but it highlights how much we can trust Jesus. As Dorothy Sayers said, "For whatever reason God chose to make man as he is—limited and suffering and subject to sorrows and death—he [God] had the honesty and the courage to take his own medicine. Whatever game he is playing with his creation, he has kept his own rules and played fair. He can exact nothing from man that he has not exacted from himself."[3] God didn't just bring us up to Him; rather, He came down to us and in so doing opened Himself to all the struggles we face. He has experienced our limitations. He's not just sympathetic toward everything we suffer, but He can empathize too.

Paul sums it up in one of my favorite passages ever: "We are hard pressed on every side, but not crushed; perplexed, but not in despair; persecuted, but not abandoned; struck down, but not destroyed. We always carry around in our body the death of Jesus, so that the life of Jesus may also be revealed in our body" (2 Corinthians 4:8–10). Because Jesus was crushed, in despair, abandoned, and destroyed on the cross, we never will be. Because defeat wasn't the end of His story, it won't be the end of ours either. We can suffer strong because we know that He's been where we are, and He will never leave us alone in our pain.

Pain with a Purpose

I moved slowly around the unfamiliar kitchen with one goal in mind—chocolate cupcakes. I slowly gathered all the ingredients and put them on the countertop. Then I combined the flour, eggs, and milk in a big bowl, looking back at the simple, three-line recipe multiple times, measuring with the precision of an engineer. An egg rolled off the counter and cracked onto my shoes. A small tsunami of batter sloshed onto my shirt. But I was undeterred. I had not had many opportunities to make something special for Jay, and I knew this would be the perfect surprise.

I filled the cupcake tins with my love made edible. Some of my love dripped across the countertop as I slid the cupcakes into the oven very carefully. Then I took a load off. I hadn't stood that much in a while. When the timer went off, my big *voila* moment was slightly deflated when I saw that the cupcakes were way too dark and crispy, but it was nothing a nice covering of chocolate icing couldn't fix. I channeled my inner pastry chef, piling chocolaty goodness on top of each cupcake. Then with a TV chef–like flourish, I placed them on a paper plate and stepped back to look at my work. Honestly, it looked like a child had baked them, or maybe even an animal. Still, it was pretty good for someone in my state, someone who just a year before was lying in a near-vegetative state, and someone who had just baked cupcakes with her one good hand literally tied behind her back.

Jay arrived shortly thereafter, surprised at my great effort and no doubt at the great mess I had made too. "Babe, why did you make these? You can't even eat them." He was right. I'd been classified as NPO ("nothing per oral") for nearly a year since my stroke. Even licking a bit of the chocolate icing off my fingers while baking had made me cough and choke. "Just because I can't eat them doesn't mean I can't make them for you!" I'd prepped and baked and iced cupcakes using only my stroke-impaired right hand. I was ready for my medal, but it was enough to have Jay taste a cupcake and gush, "Oh, so much icing, and it has a nice crispy top, just like I like it!"

Baking those cupcakes was a form of my hand-constraint therapy, which helps an impaired hand recover by making it do what it was made to do but no longer can. Naturally, the nonimpaired, working hand always tries to help too much, compensating for what its partner can't do anymore. But over time, this will cause the impaired hand to grow weaker and weaker. The stroke took all the fine motor coordination from my right hand and caused my arm to hang limp, so much so that my right shoulder stays subluxated or permanently dislocated.

The therapy first felt cruel and even a bit dehumanizing as I forced my crazy right hand to move marbles or checkers across a tabletop one at a time while my left hand was constrained. There are few more maddening experiences than the monotony of therapy, but new neural pathways can't be created without new action. Painful as it is, at least it's pain with a purpose. My therapists tried to translate these repetitions into more real-life contexts, and since I couldn't eat, they hadn't thought about me cooking. But I insisted; if I couldn't feed myself, at least I could feed the people I love.

Sometimes constraining something that already works helps something else work again. Limiting something good can help unleash an overall greater flourishing. And it did. My right hand doesn't have perfect, normal functionality by any means, but it works! That arm and hand are stronger now. They play important roles in helping me function on a daily basis. My right hand can now even carry a chocolate cupcake to my kitchen table, where I can sit and eat the whole thing with my boys. Love made edible, indeed!

We see this principle in nature often. Our California front yard was compact, but it had two beautiful coral trees that grew so big and wide in the spring that their branches created one big canopy. We would lie under them on blankets as the cool breezes of April ruffled their abundant leaves. One morning, we came out and discovered a third of one tree had fallen over in the night, directly on top of our blanket, no less. A "tree guy" came over and explained that we had let the branches get way too full and that this species was known to get too top-heavy and break in half.

"We thought the point of plants was for them to grow wild and free, and this one has been doing that!" we whined. "Every other plant we buy seems to die—apparently you're supposed to water them regularly—but I suppose since this one is outside, the sprinklers helped, and it's done what it was born to do: grow big."

The arborist was offended that we'd been all-around neglectful plant parents. "You've got to prune the trees if you want them to be healthy. It will extend their life, and maybe yours too, since trees falling on people never goes well."

The arborist proceeded to do his worst. Our once-luscious trees ended up looking naked and pathetic, like huge chopsticks shoved into our grass. It was a similar feeling to when a baby with a halo of curly ringlets gets his first haircut, but the barber uses clippers and maniacally buzzes the child straight from infancy into adolescence in one sitting. And the curls don't come back. And yet with trees, cutting back the excess allows for new parts to see the light and grow. Constraining our trees' growth made them thrive over the long term. By that fall, we were on a blanket under a smaller but safer canopy of leaves still dancing in the breeze.

Blessed Are . . .

When I think of our journey of redefining limitations, I can't help but think of Jesus' Sermon on the Mount in Matthew 5–7. He opens with an explanation of what it means to flourish, of how to be *blessed*. Suffice it to say, these "beatitudes" were not the list everyone was expecting; rather, they painted a very different picture of the good life than the one we tend to long for. Jesus said, "You are blessed if you are poor in spirit, if you mourn, if you are meek, if you hunger and thirst for righteousness, if you are merciful, if you are pure in heart, if you are a peacemaker, and if you are persecuted because of your righteousness."

To some people, these experiences may look like being cursed rather than blessed. To the world, these attributes may look like weakness and disability and being held back from living the best life, but according to the way of Jesus, these are the routes to finding God most fully. Perhaps this is why entering into community with and advocating for those with disabilities has been so powerful for Jay and me. It has helped us continue to see what the truly blessed life looks like in the kingdom of God.

We haven't always felt that way. I remember staring out the window and crying as we drove away from yet another depressing doctor's appointment. It was a little over a year after my stroke, not too long after I baked those cupcakes. We were slightly less in shock at that point, but sometimes little reminders of how things used to be, or little signs of how they would likely continue to be, threatened to take my spirit down again. A year's worth of recovery felt painfully insignificant compared to what we'd prayed for and expected to happen by that time. Reflecting on all the losses and wounds as we left the never-ending doctor's appointments and therapy sessions made me long for things to be the way they were before. Tearfully I thought, *I want to encourage people with my life. I want to tell people about Jesus. But I don't want to do it as the miracle girl in the wheelchair.*

For years after, I continued to recover, but I longed to get out of the wheelchair to find that elusive complete healing. I would mostly use a wide-base cane to hobble around in public. I just wanted to be a "normal" person and mommy again. I even set a goal to train in physical therapy hard enough to walk James to his first day of kindergarten. Thankfully, it was only a block away, but still it was going to be a huge victory. A few weeks before, I'd severely broken my leg, and I was devastated in every way. And yet we all still made it to school together. James sat in my lap and was delighted to not have to walk. And I started staying in the wheelchair more because I knew it was probably safer.

That next summer, we were invited to speak at a camp for families with disabilities. This probably seems like it would be the most natural thing in the world for us to do since we were also a family with disabilities, but I was reluctant. I worried that connecting to that community would somehow make my own disabilities that much more real and more permanent. We ultimately agreed to come and were asked to teach the group from the story of

Esther. At the end of this incredible story, on our last day of teaching, we zeroed in on a specific phrase that changed everything for the Jewish people and for us. All the odds were against them. Their defeat was imminent. Their enemies were assured victory against them. But then "the reverse occurred" (Esther 9:1 ESV).

As we spoke those hopeful words over an audience of families struggling to show up to lives they never imagined, we heard God speaking to us as well. The odds were stacked against us. There was no reason to think the end of our story would be a good one. But the reverse occurred. I had always communicated nonstop with the world, but after the stroke, I felt embarrassed to even try, since everything was so different. And yet I found a voice, albeit a new-sounding voice, to tell a story of hope to my rehab community, our circle of friends and family, and an online group of cheerleaders we'd never even met. And telling that story helped reinforce the healing of my broken heart.

When we looked up after speaking to a group of our beloved peers, our hearts broke in recognition of ourselves in that audience. We were the speakers onstage but just as easily could have been in the crowd. We had always thought about this community with empathy, but there had still been a separation between us and them. In that moment of seeing our shared story of redemption, we moved from empathy to compassion, from charity to community. These were our people. It seems that God *does* give us more than we can handle—sometimes much more. And yet He does this so He can handle it for us and so we can handle it together.

Through our bond with others with disabilities, we've seen God's profound ability to transform our minds and hearts. When your or your loved one's body or brain doesn't work as it should, the trivialities of life tend to fall to the wayside. This is both frustrating and freeing, but through the stories of our friends, we've witnessed a life that God longs to reveal to us all. It's a picture of the *blessed* life Jesus recounted in His sermon. It's the upside-down kingdom where the way up is to first go down.

It's because of this powerful experience that we decided to turn that very camp where we were once the unwitting speakers into Hope Heals Camp, which offers rest, resources, and relationships to families affected by disability. We've cheered wildly at the camp talent show as a young baby with cerebral palsy crawled for the first time. Collective tears of joy have flowed as we've listened to a teen with severe, nearly nonverbal autism quote a passage from Psalms in front of his camp family. The kingdom of God is rarely more alive than when we invite God into the place of our deepest constraints. When our sense of competency and the distractions of life are set aside due to our limitations, we can see the miracle of life in its most magnificent form. And it changes everything.

Wheelchair-Free

Now, the experience of this miracle doesn't always change everything overnight, always and forever. Sometimes it's just for a week at camp. Sometimes it's just for a fleeting moment. For us, embracing a life of disability and a community of disability has also meant embracing heartache. But this is the way of compassion and ultimately healing. This is the way of Jesus. We have been honored to enter into the suffering stories of our friends. If we have been given a second-chance voice, it's not just to tell our own story, but to help others tell their stories too. I think of our friends whose speech has been lost due to their injuries and how they invite us into a countercultural experience. It's not efficient. It's slow, awkward, and humbling. But it's an invitation to look another person in the eyes, to really see them and say, "I want to know your story. Can you help me know you?"

One such story is one of the hardest we've had the privilege to be part of. A young mom of three suffered a devastating stroke and a divorce in the same season. One of the most affected parts of her brain was her speech and language center. Despite years of recovery, her competency as a mom was still in question. As you can imagine, this particular area is a soft spot for me, so much so that I flew to her custody hearing where her ex-husband also appeared. I made an impassioned but logical plea to the judge. "If your concern is for her children's well-being, then depriving them of their mother is actually unfairly robbing them of something so valuable. Though she doesn't have all the words she used to, her life speaks over her kids even more powerfully now. What looks like a limitation will be a gift to her children. It will change how they see the world and thus change them forever. You will take that away from them if you take her away from them."

I tried to drop my mic in triumph, but it was connected to the witness stand. I also petitioned the judge for a closing state-ment, just like I've seen them do on TV, but she told me that was only for the attorneys and asked me to please take my seat. With bated breath, we awaited the ruling. Unbelievably, against the recommendation of the court's own guardian ad litem, the judge not only didn't take away shared custody time but gave more time to our friend. And in so doing, the judge gave those kids a gift that will change them forever.

It has taken me years to get to a place of contentment in and even gratitude for my limitations, but through them I have learned a new, good/hard way to live. And in the living, I've seen other people on that same journey, and it has steeled my resolve to keep living alongside them with vulnerability and joy. I smile to think of how I so desperately resisted being "the miracle girl in the wheelchair." If I wasn't in the wheelchair, I would still be a miracle girl; I just wouldn't know it.

I no longer view my wheelchair as a shameful constraint. It's no longer the painful reminder of what I can't do. In fact, it's the means through which I can now do so many things I otherwise could not. I'm not wheelchair-bound; I'm wheelchair-free. The wheelchair is the tool that helps me to be in the world again, to go farther distances than my own two legs can take me. And it's a visual reminder to myself and others who see me that I couldn't do life on my own if I wanted to, but the good thing is, I don't have to. In the kingdom of God, this seat is my seat of honor. And your invisible wheelchair is your seat of honor too.

CHAPTER 2

TELLING A NEW STORY

Redefining the Past

Jay

Every story told starts with a memory. Sometimes those memories enrich our stories, but sometimes they haunt them. Sometimes they infuse our stories with boundless possibilities, but sometimes, by comparison, they make us long for something that was and will never be again. But I'm convinced that what happens to us in life actually matters far less than how we remember it. Sometimes our memories—and more specifically, the *way* we remember them— can draw us to a uniquely inspiring way of looking toward our future. Through this lens, we get to tell a whole new kind of story and remember a new kind of future.

That being said, it's still easy to feel bitter when we aren't living the life we thought we would be living. This through line of entitlement is pervasive in our society, and naturally it deeply impacts how we think about our stories. *I deserved this, so why shouldn't I have it? I've been good; I've eaten all my dinner—so why isn't the equation working?* Or worse, *I always get what I want, and this time shouldn't be any different. Mommy, give me what I want, and give it to me* now! When we still don't get it, we start to resent anyone who was ever involved, and often that includes God, our heavenly Parent.

Legitimately, it's not just our entitlement and expectations that are the problem; sometimes it's that our circumstances have been truly horrible. Our past can, understandably, torment us. Trying to find anything good in our stories of trauma and loss can feel like searching for a goodness needle in a hell haystack. It's tempting to pretend that all is well. The only problem is that eventually we can't pretend anymore and we're left with a bitter taste in our soul that is too hard to bear. Our losses compound over the years and fill us so completely that when we look back on our lives, they are all we remember about our story.

Interestingly, Katherine and I began thinking and even researching this area of memory years ago—before marriage, before kids, before trauma and disability, before ministry, before this book was even a flutter in our hearts. We were both communication majors, which sounds a lot fluffier than it was. Our studies actually entailed a good deal of empirical research, writing, and public speaking. And come to think of it, we are actually using our college major in our adult lives—who knew?

Now I'm surprised at just how old we are and how long ago college seems. See how strangely fluid but powerfully influential memory is? I'm no longer the roughly twenty-four-year-old-ish young adult my brain sometimes thinks I am. Though if there were any major confusion about this, a quick glance in the mirror helps me remember the true story, which includes some salt-and-pepper hair and less of it but more pounds and wrinkles. But thankfully, that story and those hard-won lessons also come with confidence and perspective and wisdom. I'll take those over my collegiate self any day, but I digress.

For our senior thesis project during our last semester of college, Katherine and I paired up to research what seemed like an interesting concept called "memorable messages." I wish I could say we had the rigorous academic curiosity to have been completely absorbed by the topic and dedicated to uncovering some new aspect of it for the greater library of human understanding, but like most seniors, we were ready to be done with school and were also engaged at the time and planning our wedding. The truth is, we waited until the last minute and haphazardly threw our project together. But at least we are *both* procrastinators, and as we know all too well now, sometimes our constraints, including time, can be the very thing that helps us focus and allows us to flourish.

I studied how messages about race create our implicit racial biases, and Katherine studied how messages about beauty influence our body image. We designed questionnaires and analyzed the data, discovering just how often people hold on to negative beliefs about race and personhood and their bodies and their opinions of other people, not necessarily because they strongly believed these ideas but because they had held them for so long that they didn't know any other way to think about them.

We heard numerous recollections of how grandparents, parents, friends, teachers, neighbors, and strangers spoke an idea over them, and whether calculated or just careless, those words planted a seed in their hearts. Over years, that seed grew steadily into a deeply rooted truth with branches that went off in numerous hurtful directions. The fact is, it's far easier to find a lie and speak truth over it than to find a wound and speak healing over it. That's enough to make anyone want to put a permanent filter on their mouths. It's enough to make parents wring their hands over how expensive their child's future therapy bills will be due to all the accidental psychological damage inflicted.

What is the truest thing about our lives? Is it the story we remember and the story we've been telling ourselves forever? Is it rooted in our deepest hurts and the lies we've absorbed along the way? Or is there a truer story to be found and remembered and told—one that just might change everything?

The road to recovery always begins with the awareness that there is, in fact, a problem. *Why do I think about people this way? Why do I think about myself this way? Why do I think about God this way? Can I trace this back to a memory or an idea implanted long ago?* I think God asks us now, like he asked the first human beings, "Who told you that you were naked?" (Genesis 3:11). That is to say, "I know where your fear and shame come from, but do you?"

Here's the deal: words can heal or they can harm, and we should be careful with them and with each other. We may not be able to unhear the words that hurt us, but we get to speak new words of truth and life, maybe even shout them, praying that God will help us remember them the most. We can choose to uproot those sprawling idea trees, the ones that have been growing since childhood. It takes time and intention and help from others to rip those roots from our soil, but when we do, we get to fill the holes with new seeds and watch something new grow in the gardens of our hearts.

Of course, our memories aren't just about words but also about experiences. And sometimes those experiences are so traumatic that our brains don't even let us remember them. Yet no matter the source of our most influential memories, reframing and re-defining them can send transformational ripples across our entire being. Changing how we remember can change our identity and our future. This may sound more New Age than intended, but this truth is as old as it gets: we can't control the outcomes in our past, present, or future, but we can decide what lessons we want to learn from them. This kind of remembering is not about revising history, denying pain, or embracing an inauthentic, "head in the clouds" optimism. On the contrary, it's about a choice each of us is free to make.

For Katherine and me, much of the past decade has been about redefining the way we remember. Our story has been so, so hard, but it has also been so, so good. Remembering in its most powerful form is not about longing for the past or being defined by it, but rather about being inspired by it to look with hope toward the future. We're all storytellers and historians narrating the story of us to us. It would be inauthentic to not fully lean into the story that has been given to us—the good, the bad, and the ugly—but it would be irresponsible not to take that reality and make the most beautiful story we can out of it. It would be wasteful to not unearth the most glorious treasure we find in the darkest places of our lives and take hold of the most precious gifts we can see in the light.

Our great friend Dr. Curt Thompson put words around the importance of remembering that we will never forget. As a psychiatrist and follower of Jesus, he has devoted much of his life's work to connecting people and God to each other through the neural pathways and bodies and communities that God Himself created. He teaches that our memories are made from what we pay attention to, so what we focus on matters . . . a lot. Our brain is constantly scanning ahead to an unknown future. What will come around that corner, how will we need to react, what are the opportunities ahead, what are the dangers? Should we be afraid? Should we have hope?

The only thing our brains can use to anticipate our future are the memories of what has happened to us in the past, the memories we made based on what we paid attention to. This is very logical, so let's take it a step further. Couldn't we help our brains look toward the future with hope by paying attention with intention? Could we be less afraid of the future if we focused on the good and true and best story? In other words, could we remember our past stories in a way that renarrates better stories in our future?

To be clear, this is not about speaking our desires into a universe genie who now must make those desires come true. This is about recognizing that the brain God created in us has a profound ability to help us find Him and each other in the midst of hard stories. Our circumstances can look awful on the surface, but we can still have peace on the inside. God is inviting us to not let our most visceral, animalistic side overwhelm us with anxiety over what's ahead because of pain and regrets over what's behind. He's inviting us to pay attention to *Him* in our past stories so we can "remember" His presence in our future stories.

When this feels impossible, the antidote is always gratitude. Dietrich Bonhoeffer wrote, "Gratitude changes the pangs of memory into a tranquil joy."[4] Gratitude changes our perspective; it begins to pull back the layers of loss and reveal goodness underneath it. We need to grieve the hard story, yes. We must take as long as we need. But we need to let the redefined story be part of our grieving process, because it will also be part of our healing. And there will be joy.

La Dolce Vita

Several years into our shocking new normal, we'd experienced just enough healing to excitedly but tentatively reenter what had proven to be a very unsafe world. We'd always been active and social and loved traveling and people, but our traumatic experiences had stolen some of our pleasure in things we used to enjoy. Despite our fears, we decided to make a big memory for our thirtieth birthdays, which were just three weeks apart. We hadn't left California much in the early years of Katherine's recovery, but this momentous occasion seemed the perfect time to push ourselves with a dream trip to Italy.

Friends had offered us their vacation home, and putting countless medical bills on our credit card really helped boost the old points enough to earn us some airline tickets. Unlike trips of the past with planned activities and itineraries, I realized on the flight over that I'd only planned a few basic logistics, including how I would fit the wheelchair and our luggage into the rental car and make the home we'd be staying in accessible for Katherine. I was so proud to have packed us *both* into a single duffel bag for the nearly two-week trip, which was necessary because I couldn't drive a stick shift and the only automatic vehicles were the miniature smart cars with barely enough room for us and a wheelchair, let alone any luggage.

Upon arrival in Rome, we buckled up inside our Italian version of a go-cart and began the white-knuckled drive up narrow but stunning mountain roads, surrounded on all sides and at all times by a motorcade of Italy's widest and wildest eighteen-wheelers. And I thought Italians were supposed to be chill! You've never known true anxiety until you've driven in a toy car to parts unknown, before the advent of smartphones and GPS, while frantically deciphering exit signs in a foreign language as maniac truck drivers ride your tiny tail and hold down their horns just for fun.

When we finally reached our exit, we breathed a huge sigh of relief. Surely the worst was over. All we had to do now was get to our final destination within this ancient walled city. The streets were cobblestone and supposedly made for cars moving in both directions. The street signs were occasional. I literally (accidentally) drove down a small flight of stairs, which somehow felt appropriate. This momentous trip was shaping up to have all the heartwarming potential of the *National Lampoon's Vacation* movie.

We finally found the apartment, which had been amazingly renovated from what was once the baptistry of the seven-hundred-year-old church next door. It would have been helpful to have been figuratively dunked again, as we may well have lost our salvation on the ride over. We decided not to leave the apartment again, likely for the entire trip, as it would require more driving, and I was still traumatized.

I took Katherine's arm and suggested a walk to get some fresh air and take in the sights and sounds of this new place. We slowly made our way down a street or two, never losing our bearings— until we lost our bearings. *Hmm, I think we just make a turn here to get back, or maybe we should just loop around at this next street, which will parallel the one we need to end up on.* The quaint awnings and potted flowers and painted signs started to blend as the sun began to set over the hills and valleys. *We've survived medical catastrophe*, I thought, *but I suppose we'll just be lost forever and die in Umbrian wine country.* La dolce vita, indeed. We ended up turning the right corner at last and saw the church and found the apartment right before dark. We collapsed into bed and wondered why we had ever left home.

The rest of the trip was full of some hard moments, like missing trains and reservations, having to carry the wheelchair *and* Katherine down the subway steps multiple times because the elevators weren't working, dodging a near-fatal encounter with an espresso machine, breaking all the spokes on the wheelchair on the cobblestone streets, etc., etc. As we flew back home, we could have filled some tearstained journals with all the reasons we would never again be brave enough to go outside our comfort zones because our trip had reminded us that the world was no longer made for Katherine with her disabilities. We could have lamented how we'd hoped God would show up and give us a little boost, a little respite, or a little Italian word that means something like "carefree fun," but all we got was a beat-up wheelchair, a whopping traffic ticket for making a wrong turn, and an expensive rental car repair bill for the damage caused by my little driving-down-the-stairs incident. Who were we kidding? The part of us that sought adventure and experiencing the world was no more.

Yet instead of that journal entry, we decided to write a different one. We made a choice to recognize the hard parts, to acknowledge and even mourn our losses but to intentionally remember and renarrate the parts that helped us find some healing we were desperately looking for. Even now, when I think about that trip, I mostly remember the warm stone fireplace we curled up next to in the apartment and the smell of a real fire while cooking simple pastas and vegetables and sipping wine we'd bought at the village market.

I also remember the adventure of finding the local lumberyard where we filled the back of our mini-car with all the wood needed for such fires, which boosted our confidence in accomplishing such an earthy and basic task together. I remember seeing Katherine with spring pink tree blossoms behind her and her wonder at viewing ancient places for the first time from a double-decker bus.

And I will *never* forget how she ate, as if the culinary soul of Italy overtook her broken swallow and said, "Sit and eat, child." She spun spaghetti on her fork with delight, dipped fresh bread in the leftover broth of mussels, inhaled warm soups and fresh fish, and lingered over late lunches of meat and vegetables and wine, all grown from the same earth we sat upon. And, of course, the coffee and the chocolate knew no more appreciative taste buds than hers.

We celebrated my thirtieth birthday on Palm Sunday at the Vatican. As I mentioned, the wheelchair and Italy were not friends, so we were late. It seemed like yet another not-what-we-wanted experience might ruin what we hoped would be a special day. But when we arrived, we were directed by nuns and security guards to the very front of St. Peter's Square. We could have stretched out our legs on the marble stairs the pope would soon be ascending. Because of Katherine's wheelchair, we were ushered to the very best seats, not with dignitaries or famous guests, but next to other people with disabilities and their families. And we cried . . . hard.

The experience reminded us of how fearful we were in the world and how hurt we felt when we remembered what our lives once were. And yet now, in the soil of our pain, God planted a new story. He showed us that our weakness would be the channel through which He would show us His strength. He showed us that we didn't have to fight so hard; He would do that for us. And He showed us that what felt like the end of many things we had loved would be the beginning of a different story, of living a new and flourishing life in the same world that had hurt us.

Ebenezers

Any of us can feel better about just how not-great our memory is if we look no further than the amnesia-like memory of the people of God. At least part of the reason God chose the Israelites was no doubt because He wanted us to feel better about our choices compared to theirs! They were given an identity, a covenant, and a mission as God's chosen, beloved people. They experienced freedom from slavery and witnessed big miracles. They saw plagues brought down on their enemies, seas parting, daily manna, clouds and fire leading the way through the wilderness. And yet give them two minutes, and they'd be whining and freaking out that they were victims of a God who actually hated and abandoned them, and that returning to slavery was definitely better. Then they'd find anything, literally anything, and start worshiping it. A ball of melted-down old earrings made to look like a cow? Great idea! Oh man, they were so backward, right? How could anyone put any gods before the true God, especially when they saw amazing manifestations of His power and love?

I chuckle and shake my head as I online-shop and mindlessly scroll on my modern, melted-down metal god, now in a less cowlike shape and more convenient handheld size. News flash: we are still the people God has chosen, and we thus share the age-old penchant for pledging allegiance to counterfeit gods. We are just as prone to trade the truth of God for a lie.

Don't be too hard on yourself. God already knows how forgetful we can be—He made our brains and our hearts, after all—but He's still patiently waiting for us to remember. I imagine that's why the word *remember* is found in the Bible *five times as often* as the word *believe* and twice as often as the word *trust*. Perhaps, just maybe, God is trying to tell us something! *Remember Me. You already know the end of this story; you just keep forgetting. So remember Me.*

After generations of prophets and teachers and God's constant reminders to remember, the Israelites seemed to get it and found some powerful ways to embrace it. In their culture, remembering was always communal and embodied, meaning it required some sort of action or physical encounter or sensory experience. Those means are nearly the opposite of how we remember today, which often consists of individual reflection and fleeting, ephemeral memory devices, like saving something on our phone amid the other eighteen thousand pictures and files we can rarely find when we want them.

The book of 1 Samuel tells us more about how the Israelites reminded themselves to remember how God had worked miracles in the past. After a particularly astounding victory in battle and in the afterglow of repentance and restored connection with God, they set up a stone to symbolize God's faithfulness. They called this stone "Ebenezer," meaning "stone of help." It was a tangible reminder of how God had brought them this far. In paying attention to that reality, they could also assume that He could be trusted to take them even further in the future.

The Israelites would also do things like gather around the table to eat and share their story with each other and with the next generation, giving each listener a sense that the old story was also a new story, one they continued to live out. The traditional Jewish Seder dinner during Passover is shared to this day as a way to remember the story of the great exodus from Egypt, from slavery to a new promised land. Passages in Exodus, Numbers, Deuteronomy, Proverbs, and Jeremiah all implore God's people to "set up road signs" to help direct their minds to the "road that you take" (Jeremiah 31:21)—to literally "tie" and "bind" and "write" reminders of the story of God all over their bodies and homes (Deuteronomy 6:8; Proverbs 7:3).

We used to drive past a Hasidic Jewish community in Los Angeles where we could see immediately how committed they remain to this practice. The strings that hang from the corners of their garments help them do one thing: *remember.* People in other cultures have their own expressions of this in their clothing and tattoos, ceremonies and holidays, and ordinary use of tangible things to reveal intangible truths. The specifics matter far less than recognizing that we all need help with our memory.

When Katherine left the hospital a few months after her stroke, we took a photograph of a stack of "Ebenezer" stones gathered from the grounds of the hospital and placed on her hospital bed. We've saved plenty of other rocks from other times and places in our story. Whether literal or metaphorical rocks, what matters is to make our Ebenezers personal.

You know those scraps of paper or odd family heirlooms or small objects you got on a certain day that became an important part of your story? Take them out of the dusty shoebox in the back of the closet and put them where you'll encounter them often. Put them in a little display box or just set them on the mantel. We have little odds and ends next to our coffee maker so we can start our day remembering how far we've come. And we have that bowl of Polaroids spanning our entire marriage sitting in the middle of our coffee table. It took a while to get past the fear that they'd probably get bent and possibly ripped and be covered in sticky kid fingerprints, but when I watch our three-year-old look and see tangible memories of his own life, and life before his life, through the pictures, it's all worth it.

Despite rarely riding in actual boats and having a propensity for seasickness and skin cancer, we gravitated toward using the symbol of an anchor in our ministry's branding and in our personal lives. It's an Ebenezer image that reminds us of Hebrews 6:19: "We have this *hope* as an anchor for the soul" (emphasis mine). Quite appropriately, an anchor has a cross embedded in its shape. It has been almost Pavlovian for us in the way it evokes a positive response every time I put on my anchor socks or Katherine wears an anchor necklace or we see the spine of our book, *Hope Heals*. Apparently, it has made an impression on other people too; we've received hundreds of anchor-themed paraphernalia, from candles and napkins to bedazzled shirts and throw pillows. All of them help us remember. (And if you see an anchor item while shopping and think of us, we're so grateful, but no need to send any more. We're good.)

In 1 Peter, Jesus is called the "living Stone" (1 Peter 2:4), the ultimate "Ebenezer," and when we place our lives on Him, we become living stones too. He is the reminder of how far God has brought us and how far He'll go to bring us to Himself. We can be Ebenezer stones for each other as well. We remember our pasts and futures most powerfully when we remember them together.

We live most fully when we make memories that are illuminated with wonder and then share them. When we come together to celebrate the faithfulness of our God, we participate in the healing of the world.

There's a story near the end of the gospel of John about Jesus' encounter with His friends after they thought He was gone forever (John 21). They had apparently gone back to their ordinary lives, picking up the tattered nets they'd once dropped in order to follow Jesus. It must have seemed surreal to be back on the sea, not watching Jesus walk on the waves or calm the storms, but just fishing again as if none of it had ever happened. And it must have felt like a dream when their leader and teacher and friend appeared suddenly on the shore, calling out to them again. Jesus recommended where they should fish, and soon their nets, like their bewildered hearts, were overflowing. Their catch was a writhing, living reminder of God's provision and abundance. Someone in the group paid attention enough to count each and every fish—153 in all.

Shortly thereafter, at a beach bonfire, Jesus gave His friend Peter a gift he would never forget . . . a new story to remember. Peter, the most zealous disciple, said he'd go anywhere with Jesus, but when Jesus was put on trial, Peter denied ever knowing Him and ran away, leaving His friend to die. Peter was probably living with shame over his betrayal, shame he thought he deserved to live with forever. But as smoke rose from the fire, Jesus offered Peter Communion. As they broke bread, they also broke the hold of painful memories and replaced them with hope for healing.

I think Jesus was intentional in inviting His disciples to a bonfire on that day of Peter's restoration. Smell is supposedly the sense most connected to our memory; it can instantly take us back. I wonder if in every curl of smoke, Peter smelled his betrayal and was transported back to the place of his shame. But Jesus used that moment to enter Peter's shame-filled story, just like He enters ours, and speak words of unconditional love. Then Jesus tells us to *go* into our future, knowing we'll find God there. *Remember*— the story of love has always been the truest story.

CHAPTER 3

JOYFUL REBELLION

Redefining Celebration

Katherine

We scrolled through the online classified listings until we found our golden ticket. It was an invitation to the biggest night in Hollywood. We were twenty-two and had been in Los Angeles all of three weeks. It felt like we'd fallen off the turnip truck and rolled straight into this glamorous city. We were overwhelmed. Everything sparkled. The delicious weather, cloudless sunny skies, and cool breezes were a revelation. And the palpable sense of dreams coming alive all around us was like nothing we'd ever felt. We had arrived. And now we were getting invited to LA's Super Bowl. The national holiday for the stars. The Oscars! It was time to celebrate our first step toward all our dreams coming true.

We soon realized, however, the online offer wasn't technically an invitation to the Academy Awards, but to a party—more specifically a C- and D-list celebrity party *after* the show was over.

We'd get access to this exclusive-ish event in exchange for working for free to help set it up. All that being said, it still felt really important. It may as well have been the red carpet, considering how far away we'd previously been from it.

We drove giddily to the destination, probably with the same excitement people feel after responding to a sketchy online ad shortly before they are drugged and their kidneys are stolen to be sold on the black market. But this was Hollywood—what could go wrong? We dangled from hydraulic lifts hanging lanterns and stringing lights along the ceiling of the big party tent. We prepped incredible table displays where a feast would be served later that night. We helped bring in stunning floral arrangements and scattered them around the venue like a spring garden. It felt like we were, in fact, hosting the party of our dreams. And we couldn't wait to open the doors to all our celebrity friends. It was going to be magical.

We hurriedly went home to change for the big event. No designers had offered to dress me or anything, and somehow, despite having recently gone to approximately three thousand sorority parties and formals in college, I truly didn't have anything to wear. The difference in Deep South styles and LA fashion had already become quite apparent, but I cobbled together something festive, and Jay threw on his finest blazer. We were ready to party!

When we arrived back at the venue, it took a rather embarrassingly long time for the event gatekeepers to find our names on the party list, but they eventually let us in. We looked around in wide-eyed wonder. We'd helped make this celebration happen for all these revelers. "Hey, everyone, we're so glad you could make it!" We beamed inside. Before long, we were bumping into familiar faces left and right. The love interests in those favorite movies from our childhoods. The lesser-known judge on that popular reality show. The very drunk dude we'd seen on some commercial recently. The disco queen from a bygone era who was singing her one well-known tune in person, to us! It was a who's who of "who's that?" We would not have put them on the D-list. We would have given them an A for effort.

The night was drawing to a close, and though we hadn't been on the Oscar stage or near the Oscar stage or near anyone who had been anywhere near the Oscar stage that night, we truly felt like an integral part of the celebration. It was as if we were celebrating some future outcome, right now. There was no sense of comparison or "this isn't good enough" or "how did she get there?" or "I'll hold back and wait until it's my turn." Rather, there was a sweet sense of celebrating a not-yet reality, even when it wasn't our own night for the big win.

It was about 1:00 a.m. when we left for home, tired but wired, and we noticed another party still going on about a block away. As incredible as we thought our party was, this party had those giant movie premiere searchlights like the ones used to summon Batman. An ocean of music and laughter flowed like champagne onto the street. The paparazzis' flashbulbs twinkled like Christmas. Naturally, we thought we should check it out. It turned out that this party was the kind that didn't barter with strangers on the internet. The *Vanity Fair* Oscar party had bouncers and barricades and a huge crowd of people waiting outside to watch celebrities get in and out of the valet line. Hmm, we didn't think they'd be able to find our name on this list or accept our ticket stub from the last party, but maybe we could talk our way in! And we did.

We started chatting up a very joyous partygoer who stood near a side entrance. It turns out he was the assistant to a woman who just happened to win an Oscar for Best Actress that very night, for the second time in her career, no less. I nearly told him how I'd won Best Actress . . . in the state of Georgia in high school. But I didn't want to steal his boss's thunder. Hilary Swank was being interviewed by *The Today Show* while we became fast and best friends with her very inebriated and possibly soon-to-be former assistant. As soon as she was finished, he rushed her over to meet us as if we were long-lost cousins who had grown up on the same farm together. She was no doubt a little exhausted and confused, but she was as gracious and lovely as you could imagine. She even posed for a picture with us. Her Oscar statue was just outside the frame, hanging like a golden barbell, her arms no doubt rubbery from carrying it all night. She smiled big, and we grinned like idiots while I gingerly put my hand under her prize and helped her lift it high enough so Oscar could be in the picture too.

We floated out of there feeling like anything was possible. *Wow*, we thought, *if tonight is any indication of what's ahead for us in LA, then we're in for quite the party!* And we were, though the party wouldn't take us to the Oscar stage. Nevertheless, it would still be worth celebrating.

That night was a new way for us to think about celebration. It wouldn't just be about whether or not we got the prize but about the fact that anyone got a prize at all! It would be about celebrating our dreams coming to fruition, even if they were coming to fruition in someone else's story first. In essence, we were learning to celebrate the process way before we got to the outcome.

It's not super likely I'll ever be holding one of those golden statues with my name on it. (Though my life has been pretty dramatic and unexpected thus far, so you just never know.) Regardless, I'm so grateful I celebrated big that night as if I had won the prize. Making that kind of memory at the start of our lives together invited us into a life where celebration would be an ongoing rhythm, including when times were bad. This practice of not waiting to celebrate until we had the outcome we desired would change everything for us moving forward.

Joyful Rebellion

I remember the monogrammed linen sheets we were given for our wedding. Suddenly, I felt like a grown woman. I had really nice, grown-up sheets, and they even had my name on them, so no one was likely to steal them from me! Before that, I'd been a big fan of T-shirt sheets, and I tended to love them so much that they always ended up looking like the T-shirt a dad might wear to mow the lawn. These linen sheets were practical but felt so classy and special.

I remember unpacking them when we moved into our married housing apartment at Pepperdine. I pondered them for a moment as I looked around our dorm. *These feel too nice,* I thought. *The holey T-shirt sheets feel a bit more suited for this season of our lives*. So I took those meaningful and useful new sheets and put them on the top shelf of our closet for safekeeping. *One day, when we move into a real house, I'll use those on our bed*, I thought expectantly. *Can't wait!*

Two and a half years later, those sheets would still be lying in the top of the closet, just where I left them, while I was on a stretcher dying. As the paramedics raced me out of the dorm, our first home, the door would slam shut on that chapter of our lives, and try as we might we'd never be able to open it back up. I never saw that place again. And it would be almost nine months before I slept in something other than a hospital bed. But you'd better believe that Jay retrieved those special monogrammed sheets and put them on the bed at our first "real house" near the brain rehab facility. I got to sleep on them, against all odds, really, but why in the world did I wait?

My wise friend Sarah learned about celebrating "in the midst of" before I did. I'll always remember when she called with the news everyone dreads. "It's cancer," she cried over her dad's unexpected diagnosis. The shock and surprise of it hit their tight-knit family hard. But what they did next is something I'd never heard done before. They threw a "tribulation party" in their home that very night. This impromptu gathering was full of good food and drink and friends. It was full of laughs and tears. And the prayer throughout was *thank You*. Their gratitude was not for the cancer, of course, but they were thankful to have a God who wouldn't leave them to face cancer alone. They prayed for healing and for patience and for God's presence to be real and for faithfulness and for their suffering to be a testament to God's strength. Sarah's dad eventually survived his illness, and no doubt they threw an epic party to commemorate it. But I guarantee they'll never forget that first party, thrown in the midst, when they lifted up the God who would never abandon them.

Celebration isn't so different from worship. This is where the line starts to blur between party and pulpit. Our worship should be celebratory, so our celebrations should be worshipful. And they are because we're all worshiping something. We worship ourselves. We worship our futures and our pasts. We worship the outcomes that give us more of what we think will make us happy. But worship in its purest form doesn't happen when everything comes perfectly together; it's most powerful when everything is falling apart.

Inspired by my friend's tribulation party, I hosted a group of friends to gather around my table for a "brokenness brunch." Jay always smiles politely at my love for alliteration. I know it's kind of cheesy, but let's be honest, you're never going to forget it, and that's the point! And I may or may not have opened the brunch with a call to "celebrate God's power, provision, and purpose in the process!" Don't tell Jay.

What was interesting about the guests at my brunch was that we all shared the experience of living in a current season of great pain, but we had very different circumstances. One friend was on the verge of bankruptcy because her husband had lost his job months ago and had no prospects. Another had four kids, including one with severe disabilities that left her struggling with unhelpful systems and deep fears for his future. Another one had a mother whose ongoing mental illness had left a huge void in her heart, which was having an impact on her own kids. And the last friend was in the middle of a nasty divorce and custody battle, mired in the shame of a husband whose addictions, betrayals, and infidelity had ruined her life.

Wow, this sounds like quite the Instagram-worthy Sunday Funday, cheers-ing with the picture-perfect besties, right? Hmm . . . no, not quite. I've never been a big fan of surfacy chitchat, but seriously, who could even think of eating Jay Wolf's delicious frittata after listening to all these excruciating accounts of hell on earth? Funny enough, it ended up being more satisfying than any surfacy brunchy-poo ever could be, because realizing you're not the only one in pain lifts some of the weight off your shoulders.

When you look another human in the eyes and see how they've found strength in the face of their suffering, it makes you sit up with a little more hope. Just maybe this will happen for you too. And there's no greater way to turn a pity party into a praise party than perspective. (Sorry, but I'm not sorry about that alliteration either!) As hard as our stuff is, we realize it could be harder. Plus, being spurred to use some of our own prayers to pray for someone else's hurts is part of the answer to the prayers we've been praying for ourselves.

When I think about the healing celebrations that often happen around a table, I can't help but think of our own table, the same one my friends and I sat around for brunch (and you can be sure we ate that whole frittata, and then some!). Jay and I don't have a formal dining room table; we just have the one. It's oak and rustic and round, so no one's at the head and everyone's equally close to everyone else. It's six feet across and big enough to hold eight people, but we've squeezed in twelve when the occasion required it. It has scratches and permanent reminders of our children's giftedness at drawing with Sharpies. To this day, it's the place where we spend most of our time together as a family. It's the heart of our home. Ironically, Jay purchased this table at a time when I couldn't even eat and, more specifically, after he was told by my swallowing therapist that I would likely never eat food again! Needless to say, he wasn't really feeling that prognosis.

Maybe as some sort of act of defiance against this very real possibility or as an act of defiant celebration in the midst of it, he went out and bought our big beautiful table, the one we'd been eyeing since before my stroke. We'd long imagined placing it in the middle of our home after law school. Instead, since we were living at the brain rehab in a small furnished rental, Jay had to move the table directly to a storage unit with our other belongings, where it waited while we waited. In some ways, it seemed like a painful reminder of a "never gonna happen" future. But after nearly a year of almost daily swallowing therapy, I was finally given the green light to eat again. There have been few more healing experiences in my life than gathering around that table, eating a feast, and watching my family be nourished and loved. It symbolized a party that never should have happened but now happens every day.

Jay and I no longer celebrate desired outcomes that may or may not happen in the way we envision. But we do celebrate because, if we wait, we just might wait until it's too late to celebrate at all. Celebration can be an act of worship and an act of hope and perhaps, in a way, an act of joyful rebellion against fear.

It's about remembering our future. It's about believing that even if our plates are empty for a while, we'll still have a table to place them on until they can be filled again.

A Seat at the Table

Many summers of my life growing up, I went to Camp Desoto. I can say, without a doubt, that it changed me forever. It fostered my confidence as a young girl that blossomed into grit and grace as a woman. It wove Scripture into my subconscious through songs I only remembered in the haze of ICU when I couldn't move, let alone pick up a Bible. When I was asked in my brain rehab group a few months after my stroke to name my proudest accomplishments, I said honestly, "When I was awarded chief of my tribe and we won the camp cup!" Ahem, I'm sure my husband and child who were in that group felt slightly overlooked, but it's what came out!

Camping has played a lesser role in my adult life. I recall the two times Jay and I camped in LA in our early marriage. One time he came back with a horrifying case of poison ivy, and the other time it rained so hard that we went home in the middle of the night. God does have a sense of humor because when the idea was presented years later that we put on a camp for large groups of families with disabilities, our first thought was, *But we* really *prefer hotels!* Unfortunately, a week at the Ritz wasn't in the Hope Heals Camp budget. But what the camp lacks in thread count it makes up for in new perspective. Those of us with physical disabilities have few opportunities to intentionally leave behind our normal rhythms and move into new ones, especially within a community. In that new space, we get to see ourselves, our stories, and God anew.

We wanted our camp to be like nothing else any of us had ever experienced. We knew it would be about mourning, but we wanted it to leave us all dancing. So we planned every detail of how this immersive experience, this weeklong party, would help this whole community—from the families to the volunteers to the leaders—find the healing we were looking for. We'd have gift bags and photo booths and snow cone trucks, balloon animals and special musical guests and art installations. We'd have time for families and time for just adults and time for individuals to rest and receive whatever they needed. We couldn't bring all the women to the spa, so in one of my favorite events of the week, we'd bring the spa to the women.

But camp, like any party, can be a glorious mountaintop experience until you wake up the next morning back in your own bed, wondering if you can, in fact, get out of bed and go back to the challenges in your "real" life. We wanted Hope Heals Camp to be more than a mountaintop experience; we envisioned it as a launching pad into a new way of living in the hard life back home. So the question became, *How can we send our campers home with this perspective?*

Jesus tells a story in Luke 14 about a man throwing the feast of his life, so excited to pull out all the stops for his friends, but when he does, every party planner's worst nightmare occurs: everybody RSVPs no. Given their flimsy excuses, it seems like the host needs to find some new friends. And he does. He gathers everyone in the streets, the poor, the needy, the misfits, the rejected, the disabled, the unlovely. These are the new guests of honor. And anyone else who wants to come in is given a seat at this table. We decided this kind of upside-down kingdom party was the perfect finale to a week at Hope Heals Camp.

A seated dinner for four hundred is no small feat to pull off, and it takes a village to make it happen. We sit communal style around endlessly long tables filled with flowers and candles and wonderful food and wheelchairs and feeding tubes and wild whoops and hollers. And since no feast would be complete without good music, we are serenaded by a live concert and then flow into a dance party to end all dance parties.

Perhaps it seems strange to think of people in wheelchairs and with all manner of disabilities celebrating in this way, but it's a picture of mourning turned into dancing, of celebrating a future reality come down to the present moment. We *all* have a seat at this table, at God's table, if we're willing to be vulnerable and brave enough to sit down to the life we have and celebrate the life we can't yet see. There's a seat for you there. And you can come sit with us.

CHAPTER 4

POST-TRAUMATIC GROWTH

Redefining Trauma

Jay

If you were to sit in our living room today, you might prop your feet up with a cup of coffee in hand and look around at the scattering of art and objects. And you might wonder what story they tell about the family that lives there. You might rise from your seat to look at things more closely, to examine the book titles on the coffee table and then those on what we call the aspirational bookshelf—a few of which we've actually read and most of which we hope to get to one day when we have time for nice things like reading.

Then your eye might wander to the shelf where you'd see a grouping of ocean-colored pottery, all different sizes and shapes but the same texture and light blue-green color. They were clearly created together and made to live together, with just enough differences to make them unique and not too matchy. When you look at the final piece of pottery in the line, you might say, "That's interesting"—the classic line one utters when one doesn't know what to say without being rude. The piece was clearly pottery at some point but looks more like a hardened Play-Doh sculpture made by a baby and hidden under the couch for decades. It's a patchwork of ceramic pieces in creams and light blues and even black, sort of mounded together in a vase-like shape and put together with what looks like gold glue, which is odd because usually you want your glue to be clear and the cracks to be hidden, not highlighted.

What happened there? you'd very likely wonder. Maybe our pet broke it while we were away one day and attempted to put it back together before we returned home. Or surely there's a great family story about it dating back to some ancestor's heroic journey that brought us to where we are today. Or maybe it holds the special ancestor's ashes. "That's interesting," you'd say again, while thinking, *Why would you mess up the nice serene beauty of this place with something broken and strange-looking?*

Well, now you've asked the right question. The piece was a gift from a friend, one who had been touched by our family's story. This piece reminded her of us. "Uh, thanks, I think?" might be the knee-jerk response, but the story of *kintsugi*—this style of pottery—may be the most perfect embodiment of all our trauma-shattered lives.

This Japanese mending practice, which is quite a profound art and philosophy too, purports that an object's history is more important than its perfection. Instead of throwing away the broken beloved pottery, we'll fix it in a way that doesn't pretend it hasn't been broken but honors the breaking—and more so, the surviving—by highlighting those repaired seams with gold lacquer. Now the object is functional once again and dignified, not discarded. It's stronger and even more valuable because of its reinforced, golden scars.

What I really love about our kintsugi vase is that it consists of the original pieces—clearly not quite put back in the exact places they were before the breaking, hence the sort of funky first impression—plus a few pieces obviously *not* from the original. The new creation contains pieces that replaced parts that were too far gone or lost. The new pieces fill in what would otherwise be holes. And to keep this metaphor going, it appears that those new pieces came from other pieces of broken pottery. Doesn't look so strange and dumpy now, right? In fact, I think its unusual shape may just be the shape it was always meant to be.

Similarly, forces outside of us (or sometimes within us) break apart the world we thought we knew; yet the breaking doesn't have to be the end of the story. In our story, the breaking of Katherine's brain and body, and the breaking of all our hearts, looked like a kintsugi vase, odd in its remaking, yet beautiful. We never could have imagined it at the start, but in time, it has become a reality we quite shockingly would not want to change. The breaking of our hearts became the making of our hearts.

We often refer to the day of Katherine's stroke—April 21, 2008—as a line of demarcation run straight through our history, creating a permanent divide between the life that was and the life that is, a separation across which we can never go back. Yet those kinds of lines when ripped across our lives—scarring our hearts, breaking open our past dreams and future hopes—can with time and care feel less like chasms of despair and more like kintsugi—new vessels made with pieces of our and others' broken lives and lined with the golden hope of a God who bridges all our great divides and in whom all things, especially the broken things, hold together.

Pain and Perspective

After we got pregnant with our first son, James, it felt like our world wasn't just turning upside down but was actually imploding. We'd been married for a few years but were in the middle of my law schooling and Katherine's budding modeling and acting career. Starting a family was *not* in our plans at that time. A few hours after confirming the pregnancy, we were so dumbfounded that we somehow stumbled into a big-box baby store replete with every manner of rocking, wiping, swaddling, strolling, and burping equipment. We gagged uncontrollably while running out, and it wasn't the morning sickness talking. This could *not* be our lives!

James barreled his way into our "just the two of us" world like an asteroid. Whew, those first months of newborn and law schooling were when we began a love affair . . . with coffee. And of course with the baby too—we're not monsters—but we were *so tired*. Thanks be to God for the gift of the black gold . . . and our Baby James.

An unexpected pregnancy may not be synonymous with trauma, but at a microcosmic level, it's similar. Little did we know then that our first-time parenthood would be an all-inclusive vacation of tranquility and umbrella drinks in comparison to the real implosion that came six months later, when Katherine nearly died. But our life-altering experience of becoming parents turned out to be useful to me because it left me with a mental picture that helped me navigate the trauma ahead. A baby was earth-shattering to the world we'd created for ourselves, yet the shattering didn't mean our world or our story was over, thankfully. In fact, over time, we got to pick up the pieces together, the three of us, and form them into something totally new. Some pieces had to be let go of, but some new, really glorious ones got added, and our world and hearts ultimately got bigger. Our trauma birthed in us something more beautiful than before the breaking.

While the word *trauma* can stir deep emotional responses of despair or denial, the reality is that on some level, all of us have experienced trauma. The spectrum is so wide, and much of it, like pain and suffering in general, is dependent on our own personal experience of it rather than on the specifics of what happened. One person's life-altering trauma may be another person's baseline everyday experience.

I'll make a broad assumption that if you're reading this book, you're probably in a position of relative privilege in the history of the world, whether your circumstances feel that way or not. And compared to most of the world, your personal trauma may be relatively less acute (or it may be more). Seeing one's suffering in perspective is essential for cultivating self-awareness, gratitude, empathy, and growth outside of our tendency toward self-focus. We can't be part of the restoration of the world as a whole if we never gaze past our own navels. And a broader perspective of global trauma helps connect us to others who are also suffering horrifically in poverty, violence, slavery, and hunger, and that helps us feel less alone and less like victims.

Yet perspective can quickly go from gratitude-inducing to shame-inducing. We may be tempted to deny or diminish our own suffering because it doesn't seem to compare with the larger suffering of the world. Especially in this globalized, digital age, we know so much about how the majority of the world struggles that it's enough to make anyone lose hope for the world—and in the process conclude that their own trauma isn't worth the hard-fought process of restoration.

But here's the deal: just because your pain might not be the worst-case scenario doesn't mean it's not still pain. None of us need to apologize to anyone, ourselves included, for the stories we've been given. There will always be harder stories than ours, and there will always be easier ones. For some reason, we've been given the one we've been given, and it's up to us to figure out why and, more importantly, what we are to do with it. In the big scheme of things, our worst stuff falls under a great umbrella of all the worst stuff. That collective worst stuff was bad enough that God Himself died to make it all not so one day. Our personal trauma matters to God, because all the traumas ever felt matter to God.

As much as we need to assure each other that our unique trauma matters, we also need to assure each other that we can be brave enough to enter the dissonance of it all. It seems our modern Western culture is especially prone to pain aversion and denial in all forms. This is understandable—we're all human—but it's particularly unhelpful in communal and educational contexts that further cement the lie that pain has no purpose in an enlightened world. When our cultural centers of knowledge affirm to a younger generation that they have every right to avoid pain and shut out perspectives that differ from their own, we have a major problem. It's so much easier to sit in echo chambers where we hear only our own voices. It's so much easier to only consume media and engage relationships that repeat back to us the things we've already told ourselves are true. It's so much easier to not be around people and opinions and stories that bum us out. And yet if we remain in these comfort zones, not only do our thinking and perspective remain narrow, but so do our hearts. We miss out on the profoundly powerful experience of resilience, not despite the trauma and pain, but because of it.

Should we have to relive our trauma over and over? *No.* Should vulnerable and disenfranchised populations have to just put up with ongoing discrimination and abuse? *No.* Should we have to engage toxic circumstances or people we know are going to hurt us? *No.* But should we never enter the unsafe world for fear of the trauma it might inflict? *No.* Van Jones, a news commentator, spoke to this modern culture of fear and self-protection in the college setting: "We owe it to you [students] to keep you from physical harm, but we don't owe it to you to keep you from ideas you find abhorrent. We want you to be strong, not safe. Because the world is going to demand that you be strong."[5]

The world is not safe. People hurt each other. We cause each other trauma. And often we don't even mean to do it. Yet when we insulate ourselves from the possibility of harm, we also deprive ourselves of the beauty that our brokenness can display.

Post-Traumatic Growth

In sharing our story, we've given many people permission to share their stories back to us. Those stories cover all the ways a person can hurt—loss of a child, divorce, financial struggle, cancer, dysfunctional relationships, addiction—and naturally, many of them are stories similar to ours; that is, they're related to stroke or brain injury or disability. One thing these stories have in common, no matter the specifics, is the challenge of how in the world to maintain hope while coping with unwanted realities, even if these realities aren't so new anymore.

The wounds feel less tender in time, but they're still wounds. The memories fade after a while, but reminders can bring them back in a moment. It's a nice thought to say we should pick up the pieces and rebuild or find beauty in our brokenness, but how can we make something new when all we can think of is our past trauma? We're left struggling with fear, anxiety, and depression. Our days may be haunted by flashbacks, and our sleep plagued by nightmares. It may be hard to find a reason to go back out into the world for fear of what may happen next.

So many folks truly are suffering from what may be post-traumatic stress disorder after their lives and worlds blow up. PTSD isn't just for folks coming back from literal war; it's also for those who have fought against any of life's hardest experiences.

They may have even "won" the war, but the battle has left lasting marks on their heads and hearts that threaten their survival.

I'm not sure we had diagnosable PTSD in the wake of our traumas, but we have certainly experienced that sense of being haunted and vulnerable. In this state, we could not easily see the potential for good in the midst of suffering. But over time, we were gifted with perspective in the midst of our pain. Slowly, we began to experience the best possible outcome of trauma—namely, growth.

In the mid-1990s, psychologists Richard Tedeschi, PhD, and Lawrence Calhoun, PhD, coined the term *post-traumatic growth* (PTG). How powerful is that phrase? This theory has been researched for some time and purports that surviving trauma is good, but growing above and beyond trauma is possible. Although measuring personal growth is challenging, many people in these studies experienced resilience (coming back to their baseline) after trauma and even flourishing (improving and growing beyond their baseline) after trauma. Participants reported positive growth in these specific areas: they had a renewed appreciation for life; they found new possibilities for themselves; they felt more personal strength; their relationships improved; and they felt spiritually more satisfied. Sign me up, right?

Before we get too crazy and go marching into trauma just to get all these great-sounding benefits, it's only fair to note that not everyone feels this way after trauma. And some people who experience positive growth shortly after trauma end up experiencing PTSD symptoms later. Does this invalidate the possibility of this kind of growth? No. It just means we can't rush it. If we put Band-Aids over bullet wounds, they'll never heal right. If we rush recovery, we miss the necessary process toward the outcome we desire.

Recovery and growth are not onetime experiences. Our trajectory as humans in an unsafe world is not straight up, climbing steadily higher as we learn from past struggles. The line looks more like a bull and bear stock market—undulating, advancing and regressing. And that's okay. When we affix our lives to the way of Jesus, the traumas will continue to come; we will still move up and down on an uncontrollable and wild ride of life. But there will be a through line that brings us a blessed stability, no matter how high or low we go.

If you've experienced a traumatic experience or are in an ongoing traumatic state of life, I implore you to seek professional help or at the very least a community of empathetic listeners to walk with you through the pain and healing. There's no way around it. You have to go through it.

The same is true for trauma experienced in our distant pasts. The things we think we've long-buried have a way of resurrecting themselves at the most inopportune times and in the most profoundly powerful ways. Sometimes all we really need to do is have a proper funeral for the traumatic loss of what was before we can move on to what is. Other times, we may need to channel a full-force military attack to finally get traumatic pain and its ripple effects to release us. Trauma can draw us to fear and depression, isolation and shame, but it can also lead us to a new kind of resilience and even to an unexpected transformation.

Because the experience of trauma runs deep, redefining it is vital. In fact, scientists have found some evidence for the experience of trauma changing a person down to their DNA. This study of epigenetics further posits that a person's traumatized DNA can possibly be passed down to their children. While this is hardly proven science, we can all relate to the experience of generational bondage around abuse, addiction, and patterns of negative behavior. And yet if the negative expressions of trauma could be offered to our offspring, could the positive impacts of trauma be as well?

Six years after Katherine's stroke left her severely disabled, we found ourselves in an unexpected position: we wanted to have more biological children. It had taken years for her to feel like the mom she desperately wanted to be for James; her early motherhood had been stolen from her in a most horrific way. But despite her disabilities, Katherine had recovered rather miraculously, given her prognosis of being in a vegetative state or paralyzed or dead. When the bar is set that low, pretty much anything's a win!

God had been gracious to allow so much healing in her body and heart, and even more deeply, a growing experience of hopefulness, purpose, grit, and thriving, despite the trauma she'd experienced. After much family and medical counsel, as well as encouragement from friends in circumstances similar to ours, we decided that we can do the hard things, so maybe we should do this parenthood thing again! Katherine got pregnant, and we had John. For me, witnessing the rebirth of Katherine's motherhood was one of the most breathtaking parts of our journey.

Now, John was and always will be a kind of real-life metaphor for us. He's a picture of redemption, truly embodying the gospel message of Jesus—new life where there should only be death.

He is a picture of broken things that make new and beautiful things. He is precious and fun, so full of life, but this child has also nearly killed us both. He is strong-willed, wild, smart, and louder than any fire alarm. His nickname is "John Bomb."

Whether or not epigenetics has any long-term scientific veracity, it has been an encouraging thought to my beat-down dad's heart (and beat-down lower back) that this child has come from a mother and father who have experienced trauma and yet who have not stayed victims. John should not be here—his DNA even tells that story—so he seems to fight for and feel life in a uniquely deep way. He has grit like his mama and determination like his dad. Not a bad combo for a human to receive from their parents, but not an easy combo to parent through toddlerhood! Oh well. God willing, we'll all make it through . . . to the teenage years . . . oh, hmm. Maybe we'll just focus on one day at a time for now.

Even today, the trauma experienced by John's parents could seem like a curse, but it has been given to him with all the blessings of any great inheritance because we believe that this kind of suffering and hope intertwined has the possibility to change the way he, and we, view and live out the rest of our lives. And what could be more of a gift than to live with that kind of perspective?

No Regrets

I heard a talk on post-traumatic growth that juxtaposed the five areas of growth—a renewed appreciation for life, new possibilities, more personal strength, improved relationships, and more spiritual satisfaction—with the top five regrets people experience on their deathbeds. These regrets were collected by palliative care nurse Bronnie Ware and include (1) I wish I hadn't worked so hard; (2) I wish I had stayed in touch with my friends; (3) I wish I had let myself be happier; (4) I wish I'd had the courage to express my true self; and (5) I wish I'd led a life true to my dreams, instead of what others expected of me.[6]

The areas of growth and regret don't exactly match up, but the takeaway is no less apparent: trauma can open up a different way of living, a way that might lead to a life more fully lived and one with fewer regrets in the end. Trauma, and suffering in general, can force life's trivialities, stresses, and distractions to fall away, inviting us to a clearer view of the things that matter most.

Trauma, especially involving some sort of brush with death, can further illuminate the ephemeral and fragile nature of a life that once seemed limitless and robust. This is why growth after trauma can look like "carpe diem" rather than a cowering behind safe walls. When you've already been through the worst, what's the worst that could happen? Okay, well, you could actually die, but not living out that second chance at life becomes more fearful than dying.

Nonetheless, it seems our death-rejecting culture looks at a person's suffering, trauma, or near-death as the worst-case scenario, especially if that person is young. This is because a death-rejecting culture is also a youth-objectifying culture. So when a young person with so much possibility and vitality ahead experiences great hardship, it seems like a senseless tragedy because it appears that they lost their one shot. And that is a tragedy. Our situation was. But tragedy is not the last chapter of our story.

None of us have to be defined by our stories of trauma. This is not because we in our own strength and willpower are able to be overcomers, but because Jesus is. Faith in Him connects us to the very source of overcoming. When we have the Holy Spirit of God within us, we are connected to an advocate and comforter who speaks truth and life over our broken hearts. The resurrection of Jesus is the ultimate post-traumatic growth story. My prayer, and Katherine's, is that we never forget we are living out a second chance at life until we lie down for the final time and find ourselves gloriously renewed, not wallowing in regret but enveloped in gratitude.

CHAPTER 5

OPENING OUR HANDS

Redefining Loss

Katherine

The year 2008 was brand-new, and we gathered with our long-time small group from church to download about the holidays and dream about the new year. Someone had the brilliant idea for all of us to think about and share a single word that summed up our hopes for the year ahead. Jay and I have never been major overpreparers, so we both came prepared with exactly no words. I'm pretty sure we hadn't even thought about the assignment until we sat down with everyone that night.

Neither of us remembers anyone else's words, but we'll never forget the word that flew out when it was my turn. I wasn't sure where it came from, but it would "coincidentally" and so powerfully describe the coming year—the year that would change our lives forever. That word was *more*.

"I'm kind of shocked you said that," Jay commented as we

got in the car to go home. "It just seems a little self-centered or something. You have a new baby and a husband who's going to be a lawyer. You're already getting back to work, even modeling with your baby. Is that not enough for you? Are you really hoping for MORE this year?"

To be fair, we were both beyond ready to move on to a new season. We had just welcomed Baby James into our world a few months before. The novelty of new parenthood had worn off a bit, and we were limping a little. Jay was in the intense final semester of law school. A full night's sleep was a thing of the past. Filters had fallen out, tensions were high, and fuses were short. There was little nighttime dreaming happening, let alone dreaming together about the future or pondering a word for the year. So when I spontaneously said my word to the group, there was no doubt it was straight from my heart!

"I do think you and James and my life are enough right now. It's just that I feel deep down that there's even MORE for me this year."

Little did I know that only a few months later, I'd be lying near death in the intensive care unit with my husband sitting next to me, struggling to make sense of this insane turn of events. In light of our devastating new reality, Jay was deeply troubled as he recalled my word for the year. He reeled in disbelief, so sad at how hopeful and vulnerable my heart had been as I looked ahead to MORE in 2008. Instead, I was flat on my back, broken open, nearly lifeless, stripped of almost every good thing I'd once had. Our future was so unknown that it might as well have been lost altogether. How could it be anything other than a cruel joke to think that this year would bring MORE?

In time, over many months of miracles and shifting perspectives, we began to sense that the word I'd spoken over my life was really the word that *God* had spoken over my life. It was not spoken with cruel irony or sarcasm, but with prophetic love. It would take many years for that sense of MORE in my heart to become MORE in my head. It would take many more years before I could understand how in the losing of so many things, we would receive so many more things that we never would have gained otherwise.

It's human nature to rebel against losing what defines us. Our deepest animal urges demand that we store up anything that sustains our sense of identity and helps us keep on living into our desired future. The fear of loss can paralyze us, and redefining it may be the hardest redefining of them all. But losing something familiar or precious can also help us let go of the illusion of control and the weight of expectations that have ruled us our whole lives.

Opening Our Hands

I admit it—I'm a high-expectation, high-performing person. It's very hard for me to not know the plans and to release control of outcomes. Honestly, I hate surprises. If you want to know what not to get me for my birthday . . . it's a surprise party. As you can imagine, finding out I was unexpectedly pregnant early in our marriage was not my ideal day, though at least I could find out the sex at twenty weeks and plan accordingly. I've never been great at letting go and still showing up. But the experience of nearly losing it all has made it clear that outcomes are not mine to choose.

I don't know about you, but living openhandedly yet whole-heartedly creates a major tension in me. In fact, doing these two opposing things simultaneously can feel nearly impossible. If I have to lose, why put myself back in the expectant and vulnerable place where I could be hurt and disappointed by losing again?

This way of thinking would make sense if opening our hands resulted only in loss and hurt and disappointment, but I'm a living example that it does not. Loss is not an ending, but a new beginning. It's not just a letting go into the unknown, but a letting go into God's perfect love. If we listen, we can hear God whisper, "Now, with your hands open, you are free to receive more of Me." Our tears of loss can plant seeds of the kind of hope that survives anything.

The talented songwriter, my friend Sara Groves, penned this stunning verse in a song called "Open My Hands." When I read it, I get chills, and every time I quote it to anyone, I cry. She wrote, "I believe in a blessing I don't understand. I've seen rain fall on the wicked and the just. Rain is no measure of His faithfulness. He withholds no good thing from us."[7]

What makes these words even more powerful is that Sara disclosed her own wrestling with God's goodness while writing it. Like anyone confronted with the inevitable experience of loss—like all of us—she couldn't help but question the truthfulness of the psalmist's teaching in Psalm 84:11 (ESV): "No good thing does God withhold from those who walk uprightly." How could that be? Who doesn't know plenty of good people who have lost every good thing they ever had, including their relationships, their financial security, their health, and even their lives?

Opening our hands can be painful no matter what the loss, and excruciating when we know that things won't ever be the same again. If we don't have this, who will we be? If we share that, will we have enough left for ourselves? When faced with the prospect of losing, under the surface of our more put-together adult selves, our inner "threenager" lies on the floor in full-body meltdown, *Exorcist*-style screaming, "It's mine, and nobody else can have it!"

In the midst of her own searching, Sara was directed to the words of a sixteenth-century theologian, Sir Richard Baker, whose thoughts changed her life and have changed mine as well. He writes, "The good things of God are chiefly peace of conscience, and joy in the Holy Ghost, in this life; fruition of God's presence, and vision of his blessed face, in the next; and these things God . . . never withholds from the godly."[8]

Woo-hoo! I mean come on, that is *really* good news! Reread and highlight and write that down someplace where you'll see it every day. I think about it whenever I'm confronted with loss. All of us will lose things, yes, but we'll *never* lose God's best things for us. Jesus promised, "In this world you will have trouble. But take heart! I have overcome the world" (John 16:33).

When we get down to it, before we can truly redefine loss, we have to redefine goodness. They are inextricably linked. And like Sir Richard Baker and Sara Groves and Jesus said, the truly good things cannot be lost and cannot be taken away from us, so we don't have to be afraid. Through the lens of the Christian faith, all of this "loss and gain" business makes loads more sense. In fact, when we open our hands, God, like the most perfect parent who's read all the books and done all the deep breathing exercises ever known, whispers to us gently, "But there is MORE."

Getting to the Core of Fear

Regardless of the specific form it takes, loss is our daily reality. Grappling with this can paralyze us, but it can also free us. The neuroscientist Oliver Sacks wrote the following reflection, knowing he would soon die of cancer: "I have been able to see my life as from a great altitude, as a sort of landscape, and with a deepening sense of the connection of all its parts. This does not mean I am finished with life. On the contrary, I feel intensely alive."[9] Though not a believer in God, Sacks experienced what all humans tend to wrestle with in the face of loss: living openhandedly but still wholeheartedly. His grip began to loosen on the life he knew and thought he was entitled to. He gained a different perspective. He saw that his life wasn't just up to him but rather was interconnected to a larger story being told in the world. This made him want to keep living his own story even more—with his whole heart. It didn't make the losing okay, but it made *him* okay.

I'm convinced that fear of loss, at its core, is ultimately about fear of the big D. There, I said it, DEATH. Look, I didn't keel over. And neither will you. We can't really talk about loss without talking about death. Every day we face the possibility of death in its "big *D*" form but also in its "small *d*" forms—like the death of dreams, relationships, abilities, and expectations. Loss is unavoidable, so we may as well lay our fears on the table.

In the Victorian era, people talked about sex much like we talk about death today—very awkwardly or not at all. But everyone's still doing it, right? In our current Western culture, where pretty much every other once-taboo topic is now ordinary enough to have its own reality show, it's interesting to note that death may be the final taboo. I guess no one has figured out the most effective pitch for selling death, like they've figured out how to sell sex. Maybe it's a good thing, because that would definitely be creepy. Oh, and let's stop selling sex too. We're all better than that. Thanks!

To be fair, no era in human history has ever warmed to the thought of death. As living human beings, we're hardwired to be pretty much against it. Yet in the past and even currently in many cultures, death is more undeniable and thus more accepted as a natural part of life. In the past, many kids died in childhood. The sick and elderly were not sent away to die elsewhere. Most people eventually died at home with their families. Generations lived under one roof in a natural cycle of birth and death. (I'm still not sure how so many babies got made while everyone was living and sleeping in one big room, but no matter.)

Today, most of us would avoid witnessing the dying process up close and personal at all costs, since it reminds us that we're headed in the same direction. Talk about the ultimate redefinition! Dr. Atul Gawande wrote a fascinating book called *Being Mortal*, which explains how modern medicine has perpetuated the idea that death is a medical problem to solve.[10] Obviously, this hasn't worked out super well, because every patient has eventually died. No breakthroughs to immortality yet, but here's hoping!

(On second thought, my thirty-seven-year-old body already feels like it's eighty-seven—all that hard livin', baby! I can't imagine still rolling around in this body at the ripe old age of 237. I love my life, but Mama will be way past her expiration date by then.) Gawande says that thinking about death as something to fix and avoiding talking about it have perpetuated systems in medicine, government, retirement, and end-of-life care that reject one of the most basic tenets of life—that death is the natural end of an earthly cycle. The irony is that the fear of it actually makes people live less fully. We're afraid of death because we don't talk about it, and sometimes we die having not really lived. What a shame!

Don't get me wrong, I'm about as much of an expert on death as I am on navigating my Medicare health insurance—which is to say, it's an abyss that no one, myself included, really wants to dive into. I did come very close to death, though, and the experience left me with daily reminders of its reality in my very disabled body. Sidenote: I've always thought it was interesting that the number one fear people report—above the fear of actually dying—is the fear of public speaking. Just curious, have those of you who fear public speaking more than death ever almost died? I may be biased because I do really love public speaking, but facing death was a lot scarier!

I'm also no psychotherapist, but it seems logical that we can start to reduce our fears when we name them. "He who cannot be named" becomes just plain old "Voldemort"—we'll call him "Voldy" even—and that's not super scary, is it? (Well, it kind of is, if you've seen him.) Which brings up the point that naming our fear might also make it really, really real, at least at first. When we name it, we become more aware of what's going on inside us—that low-grade anxiety, pit-in-the-stomach feeling, dark cloud hanging over our not-quite-fully-lived lives.

All that said, we were not designed to die. We were meant to live with our Creator forever. The really good news is, if we're connected to the true source of life through Jesus, we not only don't have to deny death but don't have to truly die at all. Death may be written in our bodies, but eternity has been written on our hearts. As followers of Jesus, we need not be all that afraid of loss because we need not be all that afraid of death. We know the end of the story. *Jesus wins.*

The death of death. Resurrection. Firstborn of a new creation. Kingdom of God. Perfect eternity. Come again. A new heaven and a new earth. We get it, and hopefully we actually believe it!

That said, knowing this truth doesn't mean that our heads aren't still having a hard time with it. Right now, our living brains have never died, so it's impossible for them to get a good grip on the situation. Even though we know there's a bigger "not dying" reality, it's still a bit difficult to absorb. Even a close experience with death or a loss of a loved one doesn't necessarily equip our brains to face the fact that death will eventually be our reality too. So where does that leave us? On a lifelong quest to deepen our relationship with a God who takes our longing for human transcendence and breathes otherworldly life into it. We can move past our fear of death and loss by paying attention to the life we've been given to live now and the new life we'll have after we leave this one.

Restoring Hope

I love the picture our friend Mike Foster paints of the bittersweet nature of finding hope in the midst of loss. "Hurt and hype are on opposite ends of the spectrum, and true hope lies in between them."[11] After loss, we tend to want to either remain in our pain or pretend the pain never happened. Loss will always leave us with lingering reminders of what was and what will never be, but it doesn't have to leave us without hope. Hope is the mingling of joy and sorrow, because *hope is Jesus*. God and man. Perfection and pain.

Learning to skillfully navigate the emotional waters of loss is essential for regaining hope. While our emotions are a helpful gift, sometimes we tend to listen to them too much. We elevate their status from a useful guide to our go-to coping mechanism. I've done my fair share of scream crying, ugly crying, and silent crying, with only a few demonstrations of the lovely period-piece cry in which a single glistening tear rolls down one's cheek. In fact, over the many years of sharing our story with crowds of people, I've never *not* cried. Recounting the best and worst moments of my life to empathetic listeners always overwhelms my heart as though I'm hearing it all for the first time.

Typically, I start the crying at the point in our talk when I see the picture of my first Mother's Day, a few weeks after my stroke. Jay is holding Baby James on my ICU bed. I look awful. I don't even remember it. This is when the tears really start to flow, along with the uncontrollable snot. I have no feeling on the right side of my face, but there's some kind of ungodly storage of mucus in there, and sometimes it just slowly drips down without my feeling or noticing it, until Jay or some other horrified soul offers me a tissue. Then come the bright red splotchy skin and the swollen eyes and sometimes near-sobs. Not awkward at all, right? But at least these are real moments. I hope my tears never dry up. There's nothing worse than a canned, emotionless presentation of personal and emotional things. That's a type of public speaking to truly be afraid of!

Conversely, you may be the type of person who avoids riding the emotional roller coaster, and after my description, who could blame you? You've always just shoved your pain down deep. Too many things and relationships depend on you holding it together. Maybe you don't remember the last time you cried, and the idea of talking about your feelings with another person is as appealing as a visit to the "private parts doctor" of your choice (no offense to our wonderful medical professional friends out there). Believe it or not, I've totally suppressed my wild emotions in certain circumstances too. When things were too hard to process, it seemed easier to just not process them. Or when I was around people and places that felt unsafe, I shoved my emotions aside and put on a stoic face.

We can all fall into the trap of being all in or all out with our emotions. But either elevating or suppressing them dishonors the way we were designed—with human brains and hearts. It dishonors our communities too, because it shuts people out of our process and leaves us isolated. And it dishonors God, because we were never meant to carry the weight of our worlds; only He can. Instead of overfeeling or underfeeling, we can acknowledge our emotions and give them all to God. And we can invite other people to share in our struggles; we can download with professionals or even just share our stories with those who want to listen.

It takes time to get to this place after loss. It takes failing and trying again to reroute the trajectory of loss onto a path that restores hope. The refining process can be demanding and arduous. But we have every resource we need in God; He simply asks us to open our hands.

I have found that, sometimes, this requires getting bossy with my soul. The psalmist writes, "Why are you cast down, O my soul, and why are you in turmoil within me? Hope in God; for I shall again praise him, my salvation and my God" (Psalm 43:5 ESV). I have to keep telling myself the story of crucifixion *and* resurrection, of gain in the midst of loss. I remind myself that suffering will not take me down, because I have a hope that will not disappoint.

It took about five years before Jay and I could come up for air after we'd nearly lost it all. I'm not sure there was a particular thing that pushed us above the surface of the water, gasping and gaping at the world again, wondering if it was real and wondering if we were safe. (Sidenote: It was real, but it wasn't safe.) Our journey was and continues to be about fostering a longing for life and about seeking that life when death seems to surround us. For us, suffering strong has looked like being grateful for the things that remained in our lives in the aftermath of catastrophic loss. It has looked like surrounding ourselves with people who help call out new life in us. It has looked like researching, talking about, and meditating on the hope of a life with God in heaven one day.

It has looked like releasing our hold on what we thought we were entitled to and then receiving more than we deserve. It has looked like not waiting to live into all the good and hard realities of this life but leaning into them with wonder and without fear. And it has sounded like God saying, as He says to all of us, "There is MORE."

CHAPTER 6

FULLY KNOWN, FULLY LOVED

Redefining Failure

Jay

I'm the firstborn of four kids. I'm also the only son of a Baptist pastor—and you'd better believe "Son of a Preacher Man" was the first song we danced to at our wedding reception! These basic facts have impacted me deeply. The upside is, I had the enviable title of "Big Brother" to sisters whom I adore, not to mention years honing my leadership skills at church and home. It turned out that where I landed in the birth order made me care deeply about my connection with others, while at the same time empowering me to trailblaze my own way. Today, I'm a pretty good operator, if I do say so myself, able to effectively execute the things I feel called to do. And I certainly have a better handle on understanding women than most men!

But there's a downside to these good qualities too—like a need for control and a pressure to look good, or at least to put on a great facade. My family was incredibly loving, and yet they also, understandably, expected a lot from me. And in terms of my faith, it had been real to me since I was young, but as I grew up in the Bible Belt culture, I sometimes found it challenging to know what was *really* real. Struggles and doubts didn't seem to be welcome visitors. As a result of these issues, I came to rely on my ability to perform and achieve in order to create a persona built on one particular thing: *not failing*.

Then, in near-textbook fashion, I left for college at Samford University, a Christian college no less, and within a few months went from top-of-the-class teacher's pet with the highest moral standards to living my worst life. The pressure to perform was still there, but I was also finding what felt like freedom in finally letting down my facade.

When I first tried alcohol, it was literally a "once it hits the lips" scenario. I went from zero to sixty in one night. I was less a von Trapp teen sipping a bit of champagne before bedtime and more a fratastic idiot chugging a bottle of bourbon like water. Needless to say, it didn't go well. Somehow, I managed to still make great grades, but I was doing it while exceptionally hungover.

Halfway through college, I became motivated to make some major changes because the amazing woman I had loved since our freshman year, Katherine Arnold, was worth making changes for. Yet this path of searching for identity and freedom in all the wrong places was not easy to get off. Katherine and I broke up many times as our life choices veered wildly apart. She was heading up school organizations while I was heading to the bar. She was winning Miss Samford while I was winning chugging contests. She was pursuing her faith while I was passed out.

Unable to sleep one night, I took a drive around the nicest area of town near the school. Then it dawned on me. "Maybe some of this leftover weed from spring break would help me sleep. After tonight, I'll be done with the stuff. I'm turning over a new leaf tomorrow—no pun intended!"

I was ready for bed after my last-hurrah smoke, so I began driving home, only to have my mellow state cut short by the nausea-inducing sight of flashing lights in my rearview mirror. Interestingly, I was pulled over only because I had a headlight out (first fail). When I rolled down the window and confidently asked, "What seems to be the problem, Officer?" I might as well have been a smoky Rastafarian exhaling a hearty "We be jammin', man" right in his face (double fail). Not that I was doing much car upkeep at the time, but apparently the fabric seats of a Toyota Corolla really soak up the smell of marijuana. Have you ever found yourself handcuffed in the back of a police car scream crying? Well, I have. And let me tell you, it's pretty memorable, no matter the state you were previously in. "What are my parents going to think?" I wailed over and over.

Some friends bailed me out in the wee hours, and I spent the next several months suffering the consequences of getting the book thrown at me by a judge who didn't like his local streets overtaken by riffraff like me. To my surprise, my parents were not alerted to the arrest, nor did I tell them. I was able to hire a lawyer on my own and worked three part-time jobs, including cleaning an office building at night, to help pay what seemed like an astronomical fine, as well as the cost of the drug rehabilitation classes and court fees that came along with my life as a newly minted criminal. I felt humbled and also empowered by accepting the consequences of my actions. I felt almost noble as I tirelessly vacuumed up copious amounts of shredded paper scattered around office cubicles by moonlight. *Whew, I'm never gonna forget this one. I'm gonna make some big changes,* I thought proudly, *and no one even has to know about this humiliating chapter of my life.*

A few months later, I went off to study in Spain, quickly forgot my scared-straight vows to take the straight and narrow, and headed straight to the fiesta. Unbeknownst to me, my parents, back at home, came across pictures of me in some of my most celebratory college moments, which I had for some reason decided to thoroughly capture, have printed, and leave out in a conspicuous place in my room. (Brains are not fully formed until age twenty-five, so that may explain it.) After this discovery, they sat down and wrote me the worst email I'd ever received: "We know."

Perhaps our greatest fear is actually not failure but *being known in our failures.* For most competent people, it's easy enough to live lives of outward success. We're great at projecting an image that reflects very little of what is actually happening internally. God forbid we slip up and let some of those insides come out. What would people think? What would happen to the carefully crafted, superficial persona we've presented for so long? The fear of being exposed and truly known is why vulnerability is so terrifying to most of us. What if we let someone we trust see inside us, and upon taking a long, hard look at the messy, imperfect, failed story that is us, they say, "Yikes, I'm not touching that with a ten-foot pole. See ya never!" as they flee. The possibility that we might be known in our failures and then rejected, abandoned, and left all alone in our mess just might be our greatest and deepest fear.

I came face-to-face with that fear when I returned from my summer of fun. I was so afraid that for the first time in my life my parents would be not only disappointed in me but also ashamed of me. What I didn't know then was that while taking ownership for our mistakes is a huge part of growing up, failure's most powerful lessons are found in sharing it with those whom we've most failed, who tend to also be the ones who love us the most. When I sat with my parents in the living room of my childhood home, I felt like a frightened child, dreading the punishment that was sure to come. In a moment of grace I will never forget, my parents leaned toward me and said, "We're so sorry you made those choices, son, and we're so sorry you had to go through all those hard things alone. No matter what, we love you, and we'll always be there for you." I was exposed in my fear and shame, feeling like a fraud and a failure, and yet I was loved just the same! It was a transforming moment.

I learned that day that it's not our rock-bottom failures that spur lasting change; rather, it's finding love at the bottom *with* us that changes everything. The way forward is simple to say but much harder to live. We must find someone who really loves us and let them love all of us. It will hurt at first. It may hurt for a long time, but it will give us something no amount of successes will: *freedom*. Freedom from fear. Freedom from the fear of failure. Freedom from the fear of abandonment. Freedom from the pervasive lie that our destinies are solely up to us to fulfill or destroy.

If suffering isn't the end of our story, then failure certainly isn't either. In fact, it can be the beginning of a second-chance story. We don't have to look far in the Bible to see that it's almost comically overflowing with stories of people who failed badly, yet whom God not only loved but chose to be integral parts of His story of love in the world. Their failures made mine look like getting the wrong answer in Sunday school in comparison. It seems like a strange choice for the Bible to include all of these stories, but it also seems right to show that humans have been letting themselves and each other and God down from the start.

Not only do we read about Eve's taste for forbidden fruit and Adam's bent toward blame-shifting, which led to arguably the most epic fail of all time, but we also see disciples like Peter disowning and leaving Jesus in His darkest hours. Then there's God's beloved David having an affair with and then murdering the husband of the naked lady he creepily spied on from atop the palace roof. And don't forget Abraham, the appointed father of God's chosen people, who lied and doubted and ended up having a baby with his servant. Or Noah, who comes off an epic win riding out the flood and ends up in an epic failure—naked and passed out drunk, his behavior cursing generations of his family. And while the women then and now seem to keep it together a little better, the Bible doesn't hide major fails like Jezebel's psychotic reign of terror, Delilah's subtler manipulations and less subtle haircutting skills, and Martha's missing out on time with Jesus because she had to get that tablescape just right. And you thought *your* dysfunctional Thanksgiving dinner was tough!

Well, don't we all feel a little better? A little less worried about fessing up to our own struggles? It's not like our biggest failures were published in the most widely distributed, most read, bestselling book of all time, the Bible. It's not like our worst messes will be appreciated by strangers thousands of years from now, so they can feel less like failures compared to us. But let's face it, all of us fear failure and know it's inevitable. Understanding *why* failure is so scary and looking at it through the eyes of a loving God can make it so much easier to bear.

Expectations

Fear of failure is inextricably linked to our expectations—more specifically, to the space between our reality and the expectations we have of what our reality "should" be. It's in that space between what is and what we thought would be that our deepest discontent, stress, pain, disenchantment, and suffering lie. Sometimes the space between our expectations and reality is blessedly as small as a crack. Other times it's a chasm so wide we can't even see the other side of it.

A friend once lamented his current phase of life, juxtaposing his expectations with his reality and confessing how far apart they felt and how much frustration the gap caused him. "I had dreams of conquering the world. I imagined myself on the front of a Viking boat, fist in the air, screaming toward the epic adventure on the shore. Now I still feel like a Viking inside, but I'm driving a minivan." What a great visual of so many of our struggles in adulthood. When we were kids, we wanted our adult life to look like _____. And as adults, we often default to that childlike dream as the baseline expectation for our lives. But are we actually failing just because our grown-up realities don't look like what we thought they would when we were eight? Maybe we need to dream new dreams.

Don't get me wrong. Expectations themselves aren't bad. Our expectations are the foundation on which our flourishing in life depends. If we expect nothing, oftentimes we get nothing. As an employer, we expect an employee to do a specific job. As an employee, we expect our boss to pay us and equip us to do our work. In our relationships, we expect our friends to show up when we need them, to hold our secrets and our hands. And we place the most expectations on ourselves—to achieve the goals we desire; to be the best spouse, parent, friend, employee, employer, and human being we can be; to write a beautiful story with our lives. If we expect nothing of a person, can we call it a real relationship? If we expect nothing of ourselves, can we ever hope to grow into who we know we can be?

That said, we can get caught in viewing our expectations like a picture drawn with permanent marker, as if we could write down a future story for ourselves and set it in stone. In reality, our expectations are more like drawing on wet beach sand. External forces may come to change the picture or wash it away—and if you've ever heard the visceral screams of children when their sandcastle or sand drawing is washed away by the tide, then you know what I mean! With all that screaming, you'd think that one of them was being plucked up into the sky by an enormous seagull. Isn't that how we feel when we realize that the uncontrollable forces of life's storms can't be tamed by our dreams and wishes?

The truth is, the expectations we had in childhood are not necessarily a picture of how it's "supposed" to be. I've had a "threenager" in my home, so I can attest that what our heart and soul long for when we're a child is often self-focused, irrational, hyperemotional, and small-minded. And correspondingly, our dreams born in that time and that mind can be all of those things too.

Before you think I'm the worst parent ever to not soak up every tantrum with a euphoric twinkle in my eye, I do adore my kids. My heart stays soft toward them, even when they have absolutely destroyed parts of my home, wardrobe, car, or life. And speaking of, I would give my life for them. This is the type of esteem and connection I hold in my heart for these delightful human beings I helped make. However, I don't think they, or anyone in their stage of life, my childhood self included, should be my therapist, coach, pastor, or author of my dreams.

While it's important to maintain a twinkle of childlikeness and wonder in the midst of a hard world, we heed Paul's words: "When I was a child, I talked like a child, I thought like a child, I reasoned like a child. When I became a man, I put the ways of childhood behind me" (1 Corinthians 13:11). Now, there's a difference between being childish and being childlike. When I want my preteen to stop acting crazy, I might say, "You're acting childish. Please act your age." But then if I look at that same preteen asleep later that night with a stuffed animal or two next to him, I might lovingly think how precious and childlike he still is. Paul is simply saying that when we've matured, it's time to let go of childish ways—the self-focused, irrational, hyperemotional, and small-minded attitudes and approaches to life we naturally had when we were younger.

If our expectations aren't bad in themselves, yet the way we position our lives around them directly affects how we experience the world, then what are we to do with them? How do we let them go, as Paul encourages us to do? The answer is simple but profound: expect more of God and less of the world.

Most of the time, we do the opposite. We feel hurt by God. We don't know if He can be trusted. We want to base our expectations on something tangible, something we can control. We bet it all on a world that makes no promise to show up for us. We expect everything out of something that can never give it to us. And we build our castles in the sand, expecting that they'll never do what sandcastles always do.

At the end of the Sermon on the Mount, Jesus tells the crowd that it really matters what we found our lives on. The storms will come to everyone. It's not *if* they will come, but *when*. To build our home—which is our life, our loves, our hopes, our dreams, our expectations—on the sand will mean an inevitable falling apart when the harsh realities of the world crash in. We'll be undone by the storms and waves. Building our life on a foundation that's solid—on Jesus—may not be tangible in the ways we might desire, but it will mean a transcendent flourishing, even when the wind tears at our roof and the rain beats on our windows. We'll find our feet on solid ground that will never sink when we stand on Jesus' promise: "Expect more of Me and less of this world. You can trust Me with everything you hold dear."

There's nothing wrong with having dreams, but we need

to understand that we're not failures when our dreams don't materialize exactly the way we had in mind. Certainly, we have opportunities and skills and timing and stewardship to consider, but we don't have to be the foundation we build our lives on.

That doesn't mean we have to live in a postapocalyptic, bleak world of adult responsibilities and problems either. It doesn't mean that Willy Wonka's chocolate fountain has dried up. It just means we get to go buy our own chocolate bar now, and maybe it's dark chocolate because that's a little healthier—and we are getting older, after all. It just means that as adults, knowing what we know now about the world and ourselves and God, we have an opportunity to open our eyes to something new, to dream new dreams. And they still can be beautiful.

The Redemption of Failure

About five years after Katherine's stroke changed our lives completely, we had an opportunity to share our story of redemption and hope in a more widespread way. A friend of a friend was a book editor and encouraged us to write the story in book form (and she did the same for this book too). It felt weighty—even a little bit holy. It seemed like the next logical step in this second-chance life God had given our family. And it was a perfect opportunity for us both to unleash our type-A powers on making it the second bestseller of all time—behind the Bible, of course.

Hope Heals recounts our story from the perspective of both patient and caregiver, wife and husband. It offers a unique perspective that speaks to lots of struggling people. It was hard to write, much less to weave our very different voices together in a cohesive way. Amazingly, Katherine was pregnant with our miracle baby, John, while we wrote much of the book. The new life within her not only served as a profound motivator as we wrote down our story for him and his older brother, but it would also be a perfect ending to the book!

We realized quickly that this extremely personal expression of the most painful and hopeful experiences of our lives may not exactly stack up to, ahem, Jesus' experiences in the Gospels. *Fair enough*, we thought, *but at least we'll be able to shout out the hope and good news of the gospel from the rooftops and, more specifically, on* The Today Show. In fact, we had about four different direct connections to this beloved morning show and figured that an invitation to share our story with the masses was a slam dunk. It's gotta be hard to fill all those hours of programming; surely we can help!

In faith, we penciled in our appearance the same week our book launched. Keep in mind, no one told us to do this. We just assumed it was right and good and would definitely happen. And perhaps you know what happens when we assume things. The first week of a book release is arguably the most important few days of its life. Will it get enough attention to blast it to the top of the bestseller list? We'd read *The Little Engine That Could* several times and felt confident that the underdog in us + God's divine plan + our charisma and smarts would easily propel us upward.

The week passed with no word from *The Today Show*. "I'll bet they call last-minute to keep us on our toes," we assured each other. "What an amazing moment it's going to be when it all comes together just like we planned!" And we waited. But when we got the call, it wasn't from *The Today Show* or even the *Good Morning Local Town* news show; rather, it was from a sweet friend who owned the Chick-fil-A down the road. She wanted to host a community night to feature our book. It wasn't our plan, but it was a plan and better than no plan, so we sheepishly accepted.

It was an unforgettable evening, mostly because it was rather sad and embarrassing. But we were learning that finding love alongside lost dreams is a life-changing reality, and our sweet Chick-fil-A people and a few friends who joined us did just that— loved us so well in the midst of our unmet expectations while offering us free hot waffle fries, which may be the most winning combo ever. That said, it still felt like a personal fail as we sat next to the register on a night when apparently everyone was using the drive-through. We did sign a few books . . . for people who had already bought it on Amazon. Living the author dream, baby! We'd poured our hearts and souls into this thing we offered up to the world and felt like it was rejected by the people and places we were dying to have notice it.

Before you conclude that we're ungrateful jerks, we were and are in process. There were some things we needed to learn through that experience that have informed how we think now about our expectations, failures, and dreams. What may have felt like rejection then has morphed into what feels like protection now. Not protection from a corrupting world, but protection from a corrupting self. Truly, very few of the things I've forced to happen through my own efforts have happened in the way I envisioned. Is that failure or protection? Failure or new opportunity? Failure or teacher?

We expected the experiences of that week to mean everything, not just validating our vulnerability or offering us some success in our new endeavors, but bringing about longed-for redemption in our hard story. But an appearance on a TV show or a place on a list was never meant to give a hard story redemption. Over the years since then, it has been other people, story by story, who have offered us that longed-for meaning in our suffering. It's knowing that hurting human beings have found their own story of struggle and hope in our book that has changed our seeming failure into a transformational win.

Redemption can belong to each of us if we have ears to hear a new story. All of our failures can be transformed into hope for the future because we're God's beloved. Even though we can't change our experiences of failure and shame, we'll never be rejected or abandoned or condemned in Jesus' eyes. It's like He was away at war with our pictures tucked in the pocket next to His heart. He literally went to hell and back because we were worth it to Him. We don't have to perform for Him because He's already giving us a standing ovation. We can relax and let Him shine through us, and ironically, He shines brightest through our imperfections.

In 2 Corinthians 4:7, Paul refers to human beings as "jars of clay." I guess it's better than calling us trash cans, but it's not the most flattering metaphor! Paul wants us to remember that we're ordinary and breakable on our own, but this humble package enables us to see the treasure placed in us more clearly. We aren't the treasure; we are the vessels. But the treasure with which God fills us makes us pretty special and redeems the hardest stories. Colossians 1:27 refers to "Christ in you, the hope of glory." The divine presence in us makes us look nothing like we did before. God fills every crack of failure and hole of unworthiness with glorious light and hope. It's like we're living kintsugi pots, and our scars become golden. When He looks at us, jars of clay filled with Jesus, He doesn't see our mistakes or shame; He sees His beloved Son.

The Truth about Us

One of my all-time favorite passages in the Bible is Hebrews 11–12. It has spurred me on to persevere through painful seasons of struggle with no end in sight. It has lifted my head and my spirits to remember that I'm not alone on this journey but rather am being cheered on by those who have gone before me, to live my life well. Chapter 11 lists the inspiring faith-filled heroes who found victory against all odds, as well as the inspiring faith-filled heroes who suffered and died and didn't get the endings anyone hopes for. Chapter 12 paints a picture of this same community of wounded healers now cheering us on through our own faith-filled and unexpected journeys, pointing us toward Jesus, our ultimate trailblazer, and the hope we can have in Him: "Let us run with perseverance the race marked out for us, fixing our eyes on Jesus, the pioneer and perfecter of faith. For the joy set before him he endured the cross, scorning its shame, and sat down at the right hand of the throne of God" (verses 1–2).

We fix our eyes on Jesus now because His eyes were fixed on us all along. He already had everything—heaven and relationship with the Father and Spirit—so what joy would be set before Him? What thing didn't He already have that would motivate Him to endure all manner of shame and pain and hell? *Us.* Uniting us with the Father was the joy set before Him. We are the joy now within Him. God sees us, not with anger or disappointment, but with delight and joy. He speaks to us words not so different from those He spoke over Jesus at His baptism: "You are My beloved child. I'm so pleased you're here on earth. I'm so proud of you. I love you."

I don't know where you land in the birth order or what things happened to you along the way to shape your head, your heart, and your dreams, but it seems that no matter the shape of our soul or what motivates us to do what we do, all of us tend to look for something outside ourselves to tell us we are worthy—worthy of being alive, worthy of being loved, worthy of pursuing our unique dreams in the world. And yet we, who often feel anything but worthy or special, get to be part of a glorious story of hope, no matter what our track record of wins and losses. Because Jesus is always before us, showing us the way forward, we can have hope for ourselves. Hope for each other. Hope for the day when we'll stand in the presence of the One who loves us most and tells us the truest story about our identity: "You are worthy not because you achieved or put on the worthiest performance, but because you are *worth everything* to Me."

CHAPTER 7

WALKING AWAY FROM SHAME

Redefining Beauty

"You look fabulous. So pretty. Nice, nice. Okay, chin down. Now, um, chin up. Okay, hair down. Now let it flow in the wind. Now hair up. Give a sideways glance to your right. Give me the confused kitten look. Hmm, a little less confused. Okay, hold the pineapple higher—no, lower, lower. Nice, nice. So pretty."

I twirled around in my dress, or more specifically my muu-muu, summoning all my resolve to follow this bizarre game of Simon Says without dying laughing or losing my last ounce of dignity. The fashion photographer was a caricature straight out of a *Saturday Night Live* episode. As I paraded around a shockingly cold Disneyland tiki hut in every variety of Hawaiian-esque loungewear, I was living the dream.

This kind of modeling is called commercial print work, which means I appeared mostly in Target or department store ads. During the several years I worked in the industry, I wasn't exactly walking the Paris runways for Chanel, but since I was getting paid to have my picture taken, I was considered a working model. It was good work, but it was far from glamorous! And for every modeling job I booked, I was rejected for twenty others.

Each casting required me to get dolled up and drive within a fifty-mile radius of Los Angeles to abandoned-looking warehouses. In our first three years of married life in LA, I put more than 100,000 miles on our car driving to auditions and castings. Honestly, if I were to do the math, I doubt that my "impressive body of work" would have paid for all the wear and tear and gas for my car. But I was a model, right? I guess the question became—a model of what?

I remember looking in the mirror as a little girl watching my beloved grandmother get ready for the day. Her hands moved deftly as she "put her face on" and prepared to go out into the world. She was as lovely inside as she was on the outside—the epitome of sophistication and grace. Yet she was never without "a little bit of lipstick," even if she was only going outside to get the newspaper. I'm pretty sure she kept a tube on her nightstand so she'd never greet the day with anything less than perfect red lips! She was the quintessential 1950s housewife, complete with the dress, the pearls, and the hot casserole ready when Papa got home. Even later in life, she was always impeccably dressed and kept the same weekly hair appointment she'd maintained for a half century.

As a result of the pressures of the culture in which she lived, my grandmother found much of her identity in how she presented herself to the world. My mother's understanding of beauty and identity was a reflection of and reaction to her mother's, and I, in turn, am a reflection of and reaction to them both. I've always known how to "fix up"—I'm a woman born and bred in the South, after all—but I've never been super into clothes or makeup or hairstyles. And yet on a deeper level, I've been having a conversation with myself about beauty my whole life—one that's complex and multifaceted. Should I seek beauty? What is true beauty? Is there a healthy balance to aspire to?

I can't help but cringe and sort of giggle at another unforgettable (in the worst ways) modeling job—or should I say, not-job. I was hired to model wedding dresses for a big event at a fancy hotel on the beach. Jay and I were broke newlyweds in a very expensive city, shopping at the Dollar Store for necessities and loving every minute of it. Our favorite date night was going to a nice grocery store and eating all the free samples. So when I was told I could bring Jay with me to the hotel, not having to sneak into the pool was a real treat! Jay was in his full swimsuit regalia, ready to luxuriate poolside while his sugar mama worked inside. We had arrived.

Jay got set up by the pool while I sashayed into the lobby, feeling like Julia Roberts in *Pretty Woman* (which actually isn't the best comparison, since she was a prostitute). I was feeling confident and a little sassy, cool, and very important. When I arrived at the ballroom where the final fittings were taking place, I was herded along with my fellow lady cattle toward racks of dresses, where I quickly hopped into a stunning wedding gown.

"Can you zip me up?" I asked a waifish stranger. The zipper

stuck midway up with a jarring jolt. "Ha, that's funny. I'd better readjust. Can you try it again?" She tried again. And again. And again. If it hadn't been a $5,000 dress, I would have had her sit on me like a suitcase, though she may not have had the heft to crush my goods enough to bring the zipper all the way home.

Undeterred at this slight predicament, I approached the boss. She flipped me around, poking and prodding me like a TSA officer on a mission. Then with a look of both disgust and satisfaction, she said nonchalantly, "Since you're too fat to fit in the dress you were hired to wear, you're fired."

Shocked and ashamed, I stammered back a response. "Isn't there another dress I could—"

"Nope. Sorry. You've messed everything up now. Bye!"

The waif unzipped me; then I changed and ran out of there like Cinderella at the stroke of midnight! I was used to the rejection of not landing a job; it was just part of auditioning in the industry. But to finally get a job that seemed like a new level of validation only to have it unceremoniously taken away because my body wasn't perfect enough felt like a different kind of rejection. I admit, all those date-night snack samples and Dollar Store groceries probably weren't my best food choices, but I was a size 6 and happy with it!

I held back tears as I ran out to the pool, where Jay was already dozing with his headphones on. He joined me on my walk of shame, out of the hotel and back to our apartment. I was embarrassed and fearful about what my modeling agent would do. Would she fire me too? But Jay looked over at me lovingly. "You were already the most beautiful bride on our wedding day," he said, "so you didn't need to pretend to be one again today. Forget them!"

I tried to forget, but it was hard. It took time to recover from the sting to my ego. It took time to feel confident in my skin. It took time before I could savor the delicious grocery store samples again. I suppose a near-death experience not too long afterward helped put things in perspective just a bit, but that particular experience of rejection of my body was definitely a low point in an arena that was not only my livelihood but also a bigger part of my identity than I cared to admit. My appearance as a five-foot-ten-inch curvy and vivacious blond was a part of me that had always opened doors almost effortlessly, but after being fired for my less-than-perfect appearance, I felt fragile, insecure, and self-conscious about how I looked, not to mention more suspicious of this industry that greatly influences how we all define beauty.

That experience, though it felt shameful, caused me to think hard about the definition of beauty. Is it just about narcissism, consumerism, and objectification, or are there good aspects to the longing for beauty? Some of the experiences of my childhood and mistakes of my youth still haunt me in this conversation on beauty. And the hurts in my adulthood post-stroke have added layers of injury and insight to these complex questions. I've learned that when we feel shame over our appearance, it might just be the clearest indication that we're walking away from beauty that lasts forever.

The True Story

I'll never forget seeing my paralyzed face for the first time, months after my stroke. I'd been semi-unconscious and far too sick to move, let alone get out of bed to look in a mirror. Since part of my brain was actually removed and so much trauma had been inflicted just to save my life, the process of "waking up" was painfully slow. My brain was so foggy I couldn't make sense of what had happened to me. I had no feeling on the right side of my face and intense double vision (both of which continue to this day), so I knew something was off.

But it wasn't until I looked in the mirror that my new reality hit me full force. My face drooped like warm clay, and my right eye severely crossed in and down. It was like seeing a stranger in the mirror, which was interesting, since my face and eyes were exactly the same, except their muscles were no longer connected to the impulses from my brain. I didn't cry. I just stared, more confused than anything else. My appearance had been so important. What now?

I think our skewed ideas about beauty, particularly if we're women, are so deeply rooted that none of us have come through unscathed. So many of us have internalized messages that tell us we must look a certain way to gain acceptance. You've gotta look good. You've gotta pull it all together and not let anything bad hang out. You've gotta juggle all the parts of your life effortlessly and be a model of everything our society applauds. In other words, to be loved by others, and maybe even by God, requires that we invest a lot of effort and a lot of makeup.

I do love my Bible Belt upbringing, but Lord, have mercy, let's give ourselves a break! While these issues tend to particularly affect females, this conversation is important for men too. Men certainly can be subject to some of these same struggles over self-image and self-worth. Given the general lack of wise voices and teachers in this arena, all of us are impacted. Yes, in some ways, men are part of the problem, but by no means are they the only problem, and they are not the only solution. We need to be in this conversation together, because that's the only way we'll ever find healing. Everyone's voice and listening ear and compassionate heart are needed to move forward.

We all need to ask ourselves who is telling us the story about our beauty. Is it an industry whose sole purpose is to sell us a cure for our humanity? If companies' messages about beauty only told us how unique and lovely we already are, then we wouldn't buy anything from them! We also need to ask ourselves if we're listening to wounding voices from our childhood, families, spouses, or strangers—voices that tell us that in order to be beautiful, something must be sucked in, plucked out, or covered up.

Over the years, I've succumbed to these messages, going to some extreme measures to be thin and considered beautiful. I remember in junior high trying to make myself throw up like the cool girls did. Try as I might, my stomach wanted to keep the bounty I had stuffed into it earlier. All I could get out was a little burp. My parents tried to encourage healthy habits and accountability by dropping me off at Weight Watchers and not so subtly recommending that I walk home, but usually my big walk would stir up a mighty appetite and I'd eat 10,000 calories upon arrival. I eventually found a healthy rhythm of exercise I liked and achieved moderation in my eating. Ironically, between my impaired swallow now and the inability to be very active, gaining weight is hard because I can't eat much! I wouldn't recommend this route to skinniness to anyone.

But the longing for beauty isn't just about our faces or waist-lines, is it? At its core is the reality that our bodies will never be any younger than they are today. We will never revert to the flexibility or metabolism or possibilities we had before. Even if I didn't look in the mirror, all I'd need to do is listen to the creaks and cracks of my beat-down, disabled body. I kid you not, I've got a recurring monthly Amazon order for Thermacare heated back patches! Truly, when I had the stroke, my twenty-six-year-old body suddenly morphed into a seventy-six-year-old body. It was as if my spry, "dry clean only" earth suit fell out of the back of the car on the interstate and was run over by multiple eighteen-wheelers and then used as a bed for wolf cubs before being accidentally washed on hot and dried on high!

My laundry list of health issues has gifted me with one interesting benefit, however: no single issue could become my entire focus. My facial paralysis wasn't going to be the end of the world, because after my stroke I couldn't walk or eat either. In this same way, perhaps all of us can learn how to redirect our focus from our navels to what's going on around us, to other people, to God. Pastor Rick Warren has a notion about this that I just love: "Humility is not thinking less of yourself; it is thinking of yourself less."[12] In other words, obsessing about ourselves too much prevents us from sharing our true beauty with the world around us.

The experience of living through near-death and disability not only has compelled me to question the definition of beauty, but it also has helped me to embrace the divine love that reaches into every part of me, not just my appearance. In Psalm 139, the psalmist acknowledges that God knows him fully now and has known him since before the beginning of his life. And in creating him, he marvels that God did so with intention, excellence, and awe-inducing wonder. The parallels from that Scripture with my circumstances have been deep and transformational because my stroke was caused from a malformation in my brain that existed before I was born. I never knew I had it, but God knew. And He knew that He would use it for His transcendent purposes.

While I don't know all the answers (heck, I'm not sure I even know all the questions), I've discovered at least one thing: beneath our pursuit of external beauty is a holy longing—to be loved and desired, valued and lifted up, without having to earn it. We're simultaneously weak and wonderful, fragile and fabulous, and there's no shame in revealing that truth. In fact, there's incredible freedom in doing so. A quick look at Jesus' ministry upends our tendency to focus on the external facade to the neglect of our inner lives. He assures us that exposing our cracks won't break us; rather, it will open us to the joy of God loving us and healing our wounds. What is internal is eternal. Our outward beauty isn't what makes us worthy of love; rather, being loved in spite of everything that's unlovely about us is what makes us truly beautiful.

It's important to understand that another human being isn't required to propel us toward this beloved state. No significant other can ever love us enough to erase every trace of self-doubt. Nor is our self-love enough. Loving ourselves is a good and necessary thing, but it isn't the end goal. We can't help but be biased, fickle, and self-serving, and those are not the attributes of the kind of love that transforms us. The truth is, the pursuit of our culture's standard of beauty can lead only to disappointment in a world where everything is quite literally in a constant state of decline and decay. (Now *that's* a cheery thought, right?)

This external hyperfocus is really about trying to avoid pain—the pain of insecurity, rejection, loneliness, growing old, and the loss of abilities. Since these experiences are inevitable parts of our humanity, attempts to avoid them will leave us feeling endlessly unsatisfied and hopeless. In trying to avoid the pain, we end up making the pain much worse. The pursuit of superficial beauty and, at its core, the quest for immortality can lead only to a harsh reality: that death is closer than we think, and no magic supplement, treatment, surgeon, or prayer can do a thing to prevent it.

While I still look in the mirror and often don't love what I see, with each passing year I long for the kind of beauty that is ultimately produced only by a divine love that heals, refines, and makes me whole.

God Embodied

All that said, redefining beauty does not mean we reject the importance of our bodies. God designed them, after all. No part of us is less valuable than the others, and that includes our bodies. It has taken me many years to recognize that true beauty is the result of intentionally seeking integration of *all* the parts of who I am—my body, brain, heart, soul—and of understanding how they reflect and connect to each other and to God. Spiritual practice and formation have helped. Therapy has helped too. Learning from friends whose lives embody this kind of integrity has helped. Ironically, perhaps the most helpful catalyst for embracing all aspects of myself has been the very thing that nearly broke them all apart.

Surprisingly, the message that our bodies are or should be separate from the rest of us still exists in the Christian tradition, despite the call to follow Jesus, who is God *embodied*. We've been indoctrinated with the idea that some hierarchy of values exists, even to the point of rejecting the body altogether. We've been taught that the body is weak and corrupted and needs to be beaten into submission. The only way to achieve transcendence is to get out of it and beyond it. But think about it: if God thought bodies were precious enough not only to create them but to live in one Himself, then bodies must have inherent value. After all, when Jesus was resurrected, He didn't appear as a ghost, but in a body brought back to life.

Our bodies, imperfect and wasting away as they are, are not rejected by Jesus, no matter what they look like. Neither are our minds, hearts, and souls deserving of rejection just because we're not perfect. In fact, what is lacking in us should be embraced even more, so it can be renewed and restored at the deepest level. Jesus gave Himself for our whole selves, not just for the "good enough" parts—and not even for the worst parts, but for all the parts.

This points to another truth: the pursuit of true beauty is inherently painful because it requires sacrifice. Not the forms of sacrifice we think *we* need to make, like swearing off chocolate or faithfully attending that 5:00 a.m. spin class, but *Jesus' sacrifice* on our behalf. We can have inner beauty only because Jesus went through hell for us to get it. We don't have to pay for it because Jesus already did. We are beautiful because He made us so.

And that's the kind of beauty, in the words of Fyodor Dostoevsky, that "would save the world."[13]

When I look at my paralyzed face, I see a woman in the process of transformation. When I see stretch marks from pregnancy, I see my beautiful children who came from my body. When I see stretch marks that aren't from pregnancy, I see bountiful feasts I've enjoyed. When I see bags under my tired eyes, I see a hard-won second chance at life. When my standard of beauty is redemption, not weight; when it's sacrifice, not self-absorption; when it's new life, not chasing youth gone by, I can see there's nothing more beautiful than Jesus giving Himself away for His beloved. Dr. Elisabeth Kübler-Ross once wrote, "The most beautiful people we have known are those who have known defeat, known suffering, known struggle, known loss, and have found their way out of the depths."[14] And how much more so the person of Jesus, who emerged from the depths of suffering into a kind of beautiful strength the world had never seen—a beauty and strength He shares with those of us who follow Him, no strings attached.

Modeling Again

Four years after the stroke upended our lives, I received a phone call inviting me back to a part of my life I thought was gone forever. It seemed like a lifetime had already passed since I'd done anything other than physical therapy. And that summer, I'd fallen and broken my leg so severely that a metal rod had to be installed. Though I embraced the fitting new name my friends gave me—the "Steel

Magnolia"—more wounding was a shocking blow. Not only was it a major setback in relearning to walk, but it was an even greater setback emotionally to realize that the future would likely be full of more unexpected suffering because I was now in such a compromised state. Every day was a fight to regain what I'd lost, as well as a fight to learn contentment in my new normal. How I wished for the time when my biggest struggles were Baby James's sleep schedule and traffic jams while driving across LA for auditions!

When I hung up the phone, I smiled, then frowned, and then smiled again. I had shared my story at a few luncheons put on by the American Stroke Association, and it had been powerful for me to see my story of struggle and hope resonating with so many people. The head of the ASA's marketing department had heard my story and thought I would be the perfect face for their newest stroke awareness effort. They wanted to include me in their F.A.S.T. campaign, an acronym representing the warning signs that someone is having a stroke: Facial paralysis, Arm weakness, Slurred speech, and Time to seek help. The campaign would feature me and my paralyzed face in all its glory.

At first, this opportunity to return to modeling wasn't an obvious yes. I was conflicted for many reasons. I was embarrassed and fearful. And yet this job wasn't offered *in spite of* my imperfection but *because of* it. Jay and I talked and prayed about it and concluded that embracing this reversal seemed far more healing than attempting to hide from it. Contemplating the possibility that this campaign would inform and even help save the lives of people who had strokes, just like me, seemed like a full-circle moment.

With great love and encouragement from my personal

paparazzi Jay Wolf, I had learned to smile again. It was less ear to ear than it used to be, but it was the new me, not trying so hard to have a perfect exterior. Instead, I was finding joy in my new life and even in my new appearance. I was owning my sweet little crooked smile, which was a good thing, since by the end of that year, my whole face was plastered on billboards thirty feet tall in Times Square and on the sides of buses across the country.

When the producers of the F.A.S.T. campaign did empirical research to measure how well people remembered the message of the ad even years later, it was deemed one of the most effective ads they had ever done for any organization. Ironically, it was my biggest modeling job ever, by far! This experience helped replace the shame I'd felt over a painful part of my story with new purpose and redefined beauty.

The poignancy of it all really hit home when Jay and I spoke at a marriage event recently. We chatted with the crowd afterward, including a woman who excitedly said, "If you haven't already met someone whose life you've helped save, now you have!" This young mom had seen a billboard of my face and the stroke warning signs shortly before she began to experience those signs herself. She got to the hospital in time for her life to be saved and significant damage to be averted. Blinking back tears, I answered, "You're so welcome! All I did was have a paralyzed face, but I'm glad it helped you!" The fact that someone else's life was saved because I'd said yes to exposing my imperfection was almost too lovely to comprehend. I have never felt more beautiful than in that moment when I realized how healing my wounding could be.

And isn't this the gospel story? The God who made all things and in whom all things are held together weaves a sacred thread through all the different pieces of us into one cohesive whole. Our unlovely places become gardens of renewal and strength filled with the fruit of the Spirit: love, joy, peace, patience, kindness, goodness, faithfulness, gentleness, and self-control. And *that's* what makes us truly beautiful.

At the end of her life, my grandmother suffered from dementia. It was a painfully long goodbye, and at first it seemed cruel because her lifelong fixation on beauty got short-circuited. In her declining state, she would switch her lipstick and eye shadow. She would put on a dozen cardigans and all of her necklaces. It seemed so undignified for a woman who had always been anything but. However, in this same season, Manda also finally experienced what it was like to live a more openhanded life. After so many years of holding it together under a perfectly coiffed and polished exterior, her brain forgot to add it to the to-do list. For the first time in her life, she got to just *be*. And I had never heard her laugh aloud with such genuine and childlike delight or wonder about the beautiful world around her. She died not long ago, free from a brain that no longer worked. I'm so touched that before she came face-to-face with the truest beauty of heaven, she got a little glimpse of it on earth.

Right now, in this moment, each of us is closer to heaven than we've ever been. We're also the youngest we'll ever be. But instead of focusing on what we inevitably lose in this life, we can choose to suffer strong, growing in the kind of wisdom and love that heals us from the inside out. The years have brought us to today and will bring us to the end. We're one step closer to really living. Isn't that beautiful?

CHAPTER 8

IN SICKNESS AND IN HEALTH

Redefining Commitment

Joy

The house is dark and quiet, save for the light in the laundry room and the whirring of the dryer. The kids have been wrestled into their beds, hopefully for the rest of the night. I wish someone had wrestled me into my own bed and made me go night night, but laundry calls. Duty calls. And somehow the pile grows daily, even if I've done ten loads the day before.

I am folding tiny underwear—so, so many tiny underwear. Eventually the pile gets too high and topples over. I make an executive decision that underwear will no longer be folded but from here on will be lovingly placed into drawers in a wrinkled wad, because they're underwear and that's how they'll end up anyway.

And in one of the great mysteries of the universe, I know I

put two of these socks into the washer, but now only one remains. I almost want to slow clap in wonder at the impressive nature of this Houdini-esque feat. "Into the bucket of nonmatching socks with you," I say as I slam-dunk it. I should just throw it in the trash but don't have the heart to because maybe one day its redemption will come and it'll be grabbed from the bucket and paired with another nonmatching sock. But for now, no pairs of clean socks exist anywhere in the entire house.

Some people may view such mundane tasks with a kind of reverence, and I can do that about many things, but not laundry. Maybe it's just the daily grind of it. Maybe it's the ordinary boringness of it. Maybe it's the fact that barely a fraction of the piles consists of my own clothes. Or maybe it's just that it feels unbearable to keep showing up for the mundane, everyday tasks. Shouldn't it get easier?

Sometimes it feels like laying down our life for love in a heroic blaze of glory would be easier than the daily sacrificing of our time, sleep, preferences, and attention for the good of others. And then there are the times when it feels like there's *no way* we can keep giving our life for these crazies, much less do their laundry! Commitment to ourselves is hard enough—how many promises have you broken to you?—but how much more so to anything outside of ourselves, especially when what we're getting in return seems less than what we've been giving.

Commitment in general can be a challenge. Commitment to our spouse will always be an uphill battle, not because marriage in and of itself is so unnaturally burdensome, but because our humanity is. We are hardwired to question if what we're committing to is in fact the best we can get, or if there are better options for us elsewhere.

I remember very little about my wedding day, save for what I've gleaned from watching our wedding video on our anniversary year after year. Oh man, we looked so young and cute! After all the planning and buildup, I'm pretty sure I was just ready to get to the honeymoon. In general, so much attention gets paid to the flowers and music and reception food and the selection of dresses and tuxedo styles that will not make your wedding party look ridiculous twenty years from now—good luck on that last one. And these are not necessarily bad things. This is the party to end all parties for your family and friends, and such a kind and generous donation to the wedding industry. Yet amid all these details, something absolutely extraordinary can get lost in the mix—something that at the time I was experiencing it, I most surely didn't fully understand. On that wedding day, in accordance with law and tradition, witnessed by God and the community, perhaps the most astounding words in the history of words are spoken. And oftentimes, we in the audience or even on the stage can't help but rush through them on our way to the reception food and drink or the honeymoon. The words are, of course, the vows. Yet the truly astounding words are not the ones we think.

From the start of the idea of marriage, it makes sense to contractually connect two kingdoms or tribes or families through a mutually beneficial agreement when the terms look like these. We will be *better*, *richer*, and *healthier* together, and we will *love and cherish* each other for a lifetime. Yes and yes. Sign here. Kiss here. Done and done. But these are only half the story. Whoever wrote the full vows had something entirely different in mind, something far more stunning and valuable than health. To hear a human being covenant to another that they will in fact stay—even for *worse*, for *poorer*, in *sickness*, until *death*—should do something to our soul. Despite how some may have overlooked, mocked, or rejected these words, they are the words of covenant that God promises to us. This is not a contract; this is a commitment that will forever change everything. It's not transactional; it's transformational.

If change is an inevitable part of life, our personhood, and our marriage, then why do we expect things to stay exactly the same as how we thought they would be on our wedding day? Again, we're faced with a choice: Will we show up to a life we didn't know we were signing up for, with a person we don't fully know? Will we learn to love a different person? And will they learn to love us?

Adjusting Our To-Do List

I'm hardly an expert on commitment. In fact, I've made too many mistakes to even qualify to be a substitute teacher for the subject. Yet Katherine and I have both learned a few things about showing up to marriage and life on life's terms. Marriage may be the death of *me*, but it's the birth of *we*. It's not codependency perpetuating dysfunction; rather, it's interdependency perpetuating flourishing. We need each other.

And yet, at some point in every marriage, a spouse inevitably rolls over in bed and wonders, *Who is that lying next to me?*

We may want to run. We may want to cry. We may even want to call the police. The truth is, our spouse is probably thinking the same things about us! Every marriage is said to go through multiple iterations over the years in this process of growing both as a couple and as individuals. Add in children coming, children leaving, loss of health or financial security, changes in location or occupation—and in big and small ways we'll all be left with a different marriage than we started with.

Maybe it feels like duty sometimes. Maybe it feels like indentured servitude or even prison. Maybe it feels like a ball and chain weighing down every step. And that's why staying when it's hard requires that we make a choice. Not just once, but over and over again. But in the choosing and in the staying we will find that what once felt burdensome and confining is actually the avenue to our greatest freedom—freedom from ourselves.

The German poet Goethe (pronounced "**Ger**-ta," you're welcome) has been credited with this striking line: "Cease endlessly striving for what you want to do and learn to love what must be done."[15] Whoa, that classic Germanic resolve, hand to the plow, is no joke. Perhaps I resonate with it because I have some German blood in my veins, but more than that, I think we all deep down want someone to tell us these truths: (1) you don't have to stay stuck in the revolving door of your own strivings, and (2) you can choose another way, and in time even learn to love it. And thus at the end of our own wants we can choose to stop striving until we find ourselves with totally new desires.

The question then becomes, *What is it we strive to want to do for ourselves?* We think our to-do list already looks long, but it's nothing compared to the internal list made by the most self-focused parts of us. When we're just striving for ourselves, our to-do list will be endless. Whatever we gain in this pursuit will never be enough to fill a hole we can never fill for ourselves and by ourselves anyway.

To be clear, *not* endlessly striving for ourselves doesn't mean we neglect self-care. Plenty of us are actually doing a disservice to the loved ones we are serving by not allowing ourselves to pursue our own health. Caregivers especially—including parents of young children—are particularly prone to push aside their own needs because, honestly, who has time to go to the gym or the therapist or the bathroom when so much needs to be done? But if our deepest motivation for breaking away and resting is to ultimately return to the mess, then we can't go wrong. In fact, this is the opposite of selfish. When we "rest to return," our self-care is not the end goal but rather a means to find greater health in order to love and care for our people better than we did when we were running ourselves into the ground. You have my permission to take care of yourself and enjoy it, but you'd better come back or we'll all come looking for you!

Daily self-care and care for others are two forms of commitment, but so often what we endlessly strive for, consciously or not, are the desires connected to our oldest dreams. These may have good aspects to them, but there may also be new, deeper, and truer aspects yet to be realized. Maturity and reality don't have to kill those dreams; rather, they can be the helpful lens through which we dream new dreams.

So the second question becomes, *What is it that must be done?*

That question is both simpler and more complicated than the previous one. The answer can change as we dream new dreams, though the core distinguisher remains: the things that must be done are the things I know bring about healing and hope, not just for me, but for the person next to me, the world outside me, and the God within and all around me.

Certainly what must be done is also tied to what we've already said we will do. Commitment is about connection, and connection is about much more than a relationship with another person; it's about the integrating of all the different parts of ourselves; it's about our connection to God and our integration into a bigger story beyond our own. This is the source of our integrity. Does the internal match the external? Are we going to do what we said we would do? Is our internal life reflective of what we've presented on the outside? We are not siloed, segregated entities functioning alone; rather, we are complex and multifaceted but still able to find a consistent thread to connect all the truest parts of us. If there are disconnections inside us, you'd better believe there will be disconnections outside us. Evaluating and seeking the integration within ourselves brings all the pieces in alignment so we can more wisely determine what must be done.

And yet this still isn't a concrete answer, is it? There are so many competing concerns. Our motivations are muddy. At the end of the day, what must be done looks like loving God and our neighbor like we love ourselves, superimposing the self-striving list with a love-striving list. And yet even the cause of love doesn't always *feel* very loving. It sometimes feels like obligation and hard work. But we are not our emotions. Despite any messages to the contrary, our deepest truth is made of something far deeper than our circumstances and the often unreliable thermostat of our feelings.

Don't get me wrong, emotions are a gift to us as humans. They help us express and make sense of our lives when words don't suffice. They connect us to each other and warn us of danger we may not be fully aware of. Emotions are a necessary part of our human processing and mental health, but we need to be careful when we make them the center of our decision making.

Writing about Nazi-era Germany, C. S. Lewis warned that the Nazis may have started out disliking and distrusting the Jews, but acting cruelly to them over time eventually created so much more of the real emotion of hate.[16] This pattern seems to be the beginning of the end for many marriages. Our emotions are not disconnected from us; they are embodied in us. When we act out our emotions with another person, it deepens, validates, and perpetuates our experience of that emotion. The redemptive truth of what C. S. Lewis says is that if hate comes from acting in hate, then love must also come from acting in love. In other words, we can make the choice to act in love, even when we're not feeling it.

Cultivating a Soft Heart

Katherine and I are both firstborns. Though she is "front of the house" and I am "back of the house" in much of our lives and ministry, we're both type A, strong personalities. And we do what many married people consider their worst nightmare: work together from home. And we're not only married, but thrust into a patient/caregiver relationship as well. This combination of factors works quite powerfully for us and has been the source of great satisfaction and synergy in our life and work, but as you can imagine, it can also go really, really badly.

In case you wondered, yes, these particulars at times cause us to get into some very lively discussions and disagreements. These seem to come most often at the end of the day. Maybe we're just "tangry"—tired + angry. It seems like that should be a thing. Unfortunately, my personality type really needs to hash it all out before bed. *Poor Katherine*, you might think. Well, yes, that's true, but don't worry, you don't claw your way up from near-death and major disabilities to have another baby, run a ministry, and carpe diem every second-chance moment of your second-chance life if you don't have some grit, some spunk, and a little sass. And in almost every other circumstance, I love and respect all those spicy attributes—except, of course, when they are viciously used against me. As you can imagine, this doesn't exactly make for a calming pre-bedtime ritual.

Simultaneously, Katherine's facial paralysis requires another nightly ritual. Since her right eye doesn't fully shut, it's susceptible to drying out, infection, a cracked cornea, and possible loss of vision or the eye itself. Loss of body parts is always a helpful motivation to complete tasks. So I, with my steadier hands and non–double vision, have been tasked for years now with my wife's pre-sleep eye preparation, including rinsing out her dried eye with artificial tears, replacing the bandage contact lens, and lubricating her eye with thick ointment, as well as getting onto the floor to search for the eye mask that was inevitably flung under the bed the night before.

It's not brain surgery, nor does it require the sacrifice of a kidney donation, but it's a necessary act of love done consistently. And despite a negative emotional state, I would never withhold this vital act that my beloved cannot do for herself, nor do I run out with a door-slamming, Oscar-worthy performance, leaving her high and literally dry. Nor do I stay and perform the eye prep, adding some "accidental" Three Stooges–inspired eye pokes for good measure, or worse, some icy, passive-aggressive nonverbals that wound more deeply than any physical act ever could.

For me, the commitment to meet the needs of someone who cannot meet all of her own needs has some intense challenges; however, it has become a motivating framework in which to continue to act in love rather than out of my less-than-noble emotions. On those occasions when I truly need to choose to act in love over whatever not-totally-loving emotion I may be feeling, I take a deep breath and exhale (not an annoyed sigh kind of exhale, just a breath to get more oxygen into my brain so I can think more clearly). Then I hold Katherine's face as tenderly as I can and look at all the details of her sweet head, hair, skin, and eyes as I work. This almost always results in a little smile as I think to myself, *What a complex and amazing and stunning woman and wife and mom she is! I'm so grateful she's here with me. And I'm honored I get to help her.* Again, I say this in my head because at that particular time if I were to say it aloud, it may not *sound* particularly sincere. When emotions are high, sometimes less words and more actions is best.

In the few short minutes of internally speaking words of life about her to myself while externally living out those words, something changes. Usually the words "I'm sorry; I love you" end up tumbling from my lips. It's not magic, and it doesn't always end every conflict we're having, but it always ends the conflict inside me. God gives me a soft heart toward my wife—and while He's at it, some thicker skin too.

Perhaps you've heard the stories sprinkled throughout the Bible about what happens when people's hearts get hardened. Let's just say, it never ends well. From pharaohs and kings to whole people groups, hardness of heart is not unfairly inflicted on the innocent; rather, it's a possibility for anyone who doesn't guard their heart well. And haven't we all experienced this in our lives and relationships? Why would someone who should be loving no longer be loving to their "loved ones"? Why do we sometimes feel emotionally detached from those we should feel connected to?

A hard heart usually starts with a small hurt. If that injury is combined with emotion-driven reactions and entitled self-striving, then let the downward spiral begin. A heart doesn't turn to stone overnight; it's a process of microtears crystallizing with bitterness rather than healing with empathy. It's subtle but undeniable over time. While a wounded heart is inevitable, a wounded heart doesn't have to turn hard. But it requires intention to prevent this hardening—just as with our physical heart health—and humility to admit that such a process could even happen.

Asking God to give us a soft heart acknowledges that hardening could very well happen if a power greater than us doesn't intervene. This simple prayer can begin a humble relinquishment of our self-focus for the cause of the other. Then we can look at the world through their smudged glasses and see their perspective. We can ask with empathy, "What must it be like to be you?" which supersedes our more reactive declaration of "You have no idea what it's like to be me!"—and "I wonder what you're thinking?" replaces "What were you thinking?"

I can't help but think of Jesus' parable about the self-centered runaway son (from Luke 15), and more specifically about his older, more stable brother. Like many firstborns, he thought he'd been treated poorly by his parents, especially compared to how they treated his prodigal brother. He hadn't demanded an inheritance. He hadn't gone off and shamed the family. He stayed and did what was expected. Yet instead of healing his wounds, his grudging sense of duty caused him to do the very thing he resented his brother doing: running away in his heart. Physical staying, superficial commitment—it looks good on the outside, but it's a lie if we aren't genuinely staying in our hearts too.

Praying for softness and cultivating empathy are part of a daily and lifelong process, and it's actually how strength is found. Hardened arteries and calcification of blood vessels in our physical hearts block the most basic signals that help the heart remember to even beat. It's not so different with our relational heart. If untended, it will eventually stop working altogether.

And as previously mentioned, if our hearts must be soft, then our skin must be tough. There's no other way to protect what is now a more vulnerable heart. We are sensitive beings, prone to know things we didn't even know we knew and sense things we didn't even want to sense. But we're also miracles, much stronger and more resilient than we think we are.

Do you know the mass of details that had to harmoniously align in your body, the world, and history for you to be casually enjoying your coffee while reading this book right now? It's absolutely mind-blowing. And a marriage, this mysterious combining of two miracles into one, has to be some kind of supermiracle. We're not as fragile as we think. We may crack, but we won't break. It's not a mistake that we're here. It's not a mistake that our life and marriage exist in the world. So we need to act like God intended it. We don't have to let every careless word or irrational fear pierce our heart. It's not up to us to sustain this miracle life or this miracle marriage, but it *is* up to us to be committed enough to show up and live it.

For Better, for Worse

The process of learning to love is about being a student. We are often highly invested in filling our brains and hearts with the most meaningless information. We effectively become students of our fantasy football stats or the latest shoe sale deals or the lives of people on social media whom we will never know in person. Then we have no time or attention left to be a student of the great and wonderful mystery right next to us. What does our spouse love right now? How are they doing today? What makes them feel taken care of? Who's on their soul's board of directors? Ask. Listen. Pay attention. Make notes if you need to. It matters. And there's no faking it or cheating your way through this class.

This ongoing education ultimately helps us to know and

love our spouse's truest self. We marry our spouse's problems, but we also marry their potential. Sometimes that potential is all that keeps us going during hard seasons. We know it's there, deep down, buried beneath layers of junk. But sometimes, rather than waiting for it to be revealed, we take it upon ourselves to put on a hazmat suit and get in there. It's up to us! We know we've got the formula. We know we can make the changes needed to get our spouse's truest self unearthed and living that best life.

But being the agent of change never goes very well. In fact, we put ourselves in a position we were never meant to be in, heaped with expectations we were never meant to bear. If we can't change them, then they never will. But what if we weren't meant to change them? What if we were meant to know them and love them and see the truest version of them, the one even they can't fully see? What if instead of the change agent, we were the cheerleader? Relentlessly hopeful, endlessly encouraging, expecting change to come from God and not from us. And in so doing, we may gain our own cheerleader for life in them as well.

At twenty-two, my underdeveloped brain didn't know what it was promising when I married Katherine. But I do know I promised to do something I still intend to do, even if I didn't fully understand what I was promising at the time. How in the world could I ever have imagined what I was actually signing up for? How could I have known that under Katherine's veil, deep inside her brain, was an unknown neurovascular issue that would change everything just three and a half years later? Yet every marriage experiences this exact same thing. We promise to spend an unknown future with an unknown partner. And make no mistake, in our marriage, this naive vowing went both ways. Katherine didn't fully know what she was getting into. She didn't fully know me because I didn't even fully know myself then. She was committing to all my past and all my future—the person I was and the person I would become.

Every marriage promises our lives and futures, the best and worst possibilities, to another person whom we can never fully know at the time of the promise. Yet the unknown doesn't invalidate the promise. Even the nondisclosure of the known doesn't invalidate the promise. If marriage were simply a contract, then it could be effectively argued that this is not what I signed up for, so I don't have to stay. Instead, marriage is a safe setting for a wild love to find its peace unconditionally. The goal of this kind of commitment is not mutual happiness or a secure future; it's not conditional based on circumstances foreseen or unforeseen. Rather, the goal of marriage is to be fully known and fully loved at the very same time. It's no coincidence that this is also the goal of a true relationship with God.

I'm a big fan of marriage and staying in marriage, especially when it gets hard. And I'm the humble recipient of my wife's gospel-inspired forgiveness and unconditional love too. Marriage can make space for redemption of our worst, healing of our wounds, and hope for our best. Yet sadly, in all kinds of crafty ways, humans, and even humans professing to follow Jesus, have used the idea of this unconditional promise for their own benefit. Abuse and abandonment, dysfunction and manipulation, have been permitted under the guise of commitment. And I've also seen spouses dragging entirely dead parts of their relationship like in a zombie apocalypse as they try desperately to convince themselves and everyone else that everything's fine. Dead things need to be buried before there's any hope of them being resurrected. Thankfully, if we know Jesus, we know He's all about offering life where there should only be death.

I don't know your life. I don't know the specifics of your story. I don't know what is in fact wounded or what is dead, but I encourage you to find someone who does. Get a therapist or pastor or confidant who can counsel you on finding health and life in your relationship. This doesn't mean that vulnerability won't cause ripple effects. This doesn't mean that a new awareness of old wounds won't cause deeper wounds for a time. This doesn't mean that fully knowing and unconditionally loving will be a walk in the park. It just means that there is healing to be done together within the safe and strong walls of a covenant lived out in community. And if the marriage foundation is built on Jesus, then no storm can take down that house. Dietrich Bonhoeffer wrote a marriage sermon culminating in this poignant idea: that although love had brought this couple together, even to that wedding day, ultimately, "It is not your love that sustains the marriage, but from now on, the marriage that sustains your love."[17]

Did I stay in my marriage after everything changed? *Yes.* Has the marriage and the staying and the struggle been one of the hardest things I've ever done? *Yes.* But has it forever changed the way I see myself, others, and God? *Yes.* And is it worth it to stay? *Yes. Yes.* And *YES.* Welcome to how God experiences His relationship with us! Yet God commits to us not because we can ever equally commit to Him but because He loves us so much

He's not even measuring. When we bring this perspective to our marriages, something profound takes place. We stop measuring love and start choosing love. And if our daily recommittal offering of self is ultimately to God, whom we can't outgive or repay, and not our spouse, then we'll never end up feeling like we got the short end of the stick. We'll feel like we got more than we could ever deserve.

The last load of laundry is nearly finished, and honestly, it smells quite nice. Maybe I'm delirious. On this cold winter night, I think I can smell the beach in late summer. It's heaven. Maybe it's a waking dream. Or maybe it's just the expensive essential oil detergent, but wow, this moment confirms that it's worth every penny. As I pull out the sheets for our bed, they instantly surround me with warmth. I feel like I'm in a TV commercial, except our laundry room isn't big enough for a slow-motion unfurling of the sheets. I try this move and nearly whip down the overhead light fixture. Nonetheless, I'm having a moment. Though I won't begin to attempt a neat fold of the fitted sheet (that's Martha Stewart–level stuff), somehow this everyday experience feels a little more sacred. I get a glimpse and smell and touch of how this sometimes burdensome work matters, not just to my people, but to me. It will be part of giving them a clean and safe and incredible smelling place to rest . . . but I'll get to rest there too.

Tonight Katherine helps make the bed with me. We stretch and tuck and smooth the clean white sheets, doing that annoying tug-of-war thing when two people make a bed, but remembering how much easier it is to make a bed together rather than solo. We fluff-beat the pillows for good measure, taking out some minor laundry-related aggression, and do a big exhale before we climb in. There's nothing like that feeling of sliding your feet into fresh sheets, especially when you know they'll probably be dirty by the next night because a child spilled or smeared something that's just too gross to sleep on. But there is truly nothing like that feeling of sliding your feet against the feet next to yours, cold as they may be, knowing they're worth every minute of laboring over laundry—and anything else, for that matter. For now, the mundane messiness that marriage often requires is forgotten. For now, we rest in the scent of sea-salt sheets and hard-won love. And tomorrow we'll wake up, God willing, and do it all over again.

CHAPTER 9

THE POWER OF "WE"

Redefining Community

We piled out of the dated stretch limo, adjusting our wedding attire and laughing nervously as we stood in front of the famous little white chapel in Las Vegas. It wouldn't be the first walk down the aisle for Jay and me, nor for our friends, but it would be the first time we'd done it together—not to mention the first time we'd done it with Elvis serenading us.

Our small group of five couples from church had known each other for years, and we'd forged strong bonds as we struggled and celebrated through young-married life in Los Angeles. We continued to gather weekly, even when some couples moved to different churches or different parts of the city. And perhaps most importantly, we continued to meet when faced with life-changing circumstances, new babies, divorce, dysfunction, and near-death. The group had morphed over time, particularly through the hardships, to become a family. Like most families, we didn't all agree on everything. We hurt each other's feelings sometimes. We grew closer in some seasons, and apart in others. Yet we had chosen to be in community, and the experience of choosing again and again over the years, especially through suffering, created a bond that none of us had ever known before.

To honor all the ways in which this long-standing community had helped strengthen each of our marriages, we decided to celebrate with a vow renewal in Vegas. Ten people doing life together for seven years, with nearly fifty years of marriage between us, with one Groupon for an "Impromptu Vegas Elopement," seven kids in tow, my eight-dollar, thrift-store vintage dress (of which I was super proud), two pregnant brides, and one Elvis impersonator combined to deliver an unforgettable experience. The officiant, a retired pastor, wasn't used to sober wedding parties, much less ones in which all the participants knew each other. When he heard the story of our struggles and hopes, near-death and new life, all lived out together over nearly a decade, he wept. And at the close of the ceremony, as we all danced to Elvis singing "I can't help falling in love with you," tears of gratitude flowed from each of us. Where would we be without each other? God only knows.

As human beings, we're all hardwired for connection. We long to find a place where we can love and be loved, know and be known, offer our unique gifts and receive different gifts in return. As researcher and storyteller Brené Brown writes, "A deep sense of love and belonging is an irreducible need of all women, men, and children . . . When those needs are not met, we don't function as we were meant to. We break. We fall apart. We numb.

We ache. We hurt others. We get sick . . . The absence of love and belonging will always lead to suffering."[18]

Jay and I have learned that in the process of being redefined in the midst of suffering, community is not just another item on the list to redefine, but rather it's the scaffolding around the whole process of transformation. When I had the stroke, we were reading Bonhoeffer's *Life Together* in our small group. It was a stunningly timed springboard from which our concept of community jumped from theory to hard-won reality. These devoted friends kept vigil, shifting their lives and schedules to sit in hospital waiting rooms for weeks and months. Throughout that time, everyone offered their unique gifts to whoever was struggling. Like the earliest form of the Christian church, when there was a need in the group, resources were offered to meet the need. It was a powerful demonstration of how the church should be functioning today. So many strangers witnessed this large and tireless group surrounding our family and asked how they could be part of something like that themselves.

The journey of redefining loss and gain and goodness was never meant to be undertaken alone. It was meant to be wrestled with and learned alongside people trying to do the same thing. It's natural to isolate ourselves when we're afraid, or to stop putting ourselves out there in the world when we've lost something precious. And certainly there is a time and place for private grief, for making personal space to start the healing process.

After my stroke, it took months before I was physically well enough to even go outside the hospital, but it took many more months after that to be emotionally well enough to go back to church. To be truly seen and known in the midst of my losses

145

made them that much more real. But waiting until I was fully healed and feeling great to rejoin my community would have been a big mistake. If I'd waited to come back until some future milestone was reached, I may have found myself a long way down the road, feeling alone and bitter and still not feeling healed or great. Instead, when I wrestled with my new normal in the context of community, the struggle became part of our story—not only of my suffering, but of the power of community in general. Now when someone else in our group experiences loss, they're more likely to come back and get everything they need because they know that's what happened for me.

Better Together

Quite appropriately, so many of the thoughts on the pages of this book were forged in a gathering for women I led about five years after my stroke. I had a deep sense that the rumblings unearthed in my heart throughout the years of processing my journey needed to be thought out and then shared. Continuing to deepen my experience of community actually redefined it for me in some ways. As valuable as my connection with others has been throughout my life, I came to appreciate it more and more as the people God placed in my California circle helped me to suffer strong.

As I've mentioned, I'm a big fan of alliteration, but a close second are acronyms (cue the eye roll from Jay Wolf). I branded this gathering MORE (remember that story about my word for 2008?), and it stood for "Mornings of Redefining Everything." I insisted that we gather early on Saturday mornings, when husbands and kids were still sleeping and our brains were fuzzy enough to be receptive to all the redefining. I also insisted that due to the early hour and my general aversion to major primping, each woman would come dressed in her finest pajama ensemble. Sometimes the top knots and eyeglasses and coffee knew no bounds as nearly one hundred women rolled up from all over the city, looking for God and finding Him together. During the four years I gathered with those women, I experienced so much healing.

In an earlier chapter, Jay talked about the impact that memory has in redefining the past and anticipating the future with refined faith. It's not surprising that when we're in a communal setting, we can remember together better than we can alone. Psychologists call this "integration," which is such a hopeful picture of the strength found in interconnectedness—much preferable to its alternative, *dis*integration. Integration certainly happens individually within ourselves and with ourselves and God, but it was never meant to stay inside us. The poet Mary Oliver writes, "Instructions for living a life: *Pay attention. Be astonished. Tell about it.*"[19]

When we come together, we get to remind each other that stories that feel so personal are actually so universal. In fact, studies of the impact of close connections with others during periods of acute stress reveal that recovery is strongly influenced by one's connection to and support from his or her community. Trauma is a personal experience, but recovery is a communal one. It's essential that we invite others into our traumas and the process of recovering from them. Moreover, it's critical that we renarrate our stories in light of this communal recovery.

A fascinating study by James Pennebaker analyzed the pronouns used in people's personal reflections of coping with loss.[20] He found that participants who more often used the pronoun "we" than "I" later reported some version of post-traumatic growth. He even did the same linguistic inquiry on famous poets and found that the ones who more often used "I" words were also more likely to take their own lives.[21] Embracing the option of "we" instead of trying to go it alone can help us detach from some of the personal sting of our trauma and see it in light of a greater story of healing and hope in the world. It can help us in the process of rebuilding what's been shattered and starting to live into something totally different. It's no small task, and it will take as long as it takes, but *we've got this* because *we've got each other*!

Compassion

Jay and I have found that our deepest healing comes when we're part of someone else's healing. I've been shocked at times to find that the very place of my wounding becomes the place of someone else's healing. Yet I really shouldn't be surprised; God wants to heal the world, and healing in every microcosmic sense plays a vital role in His grand story.

Becoming part of that story requires that we have compassion for each other in the midst of difficult journeys. Compassion literally means "with suffering" (like "the passion of Christ" associated with Jesus' crucifixion). Unfortunately, the word *compassion* has become rather watered down in its modern usage, yet we see throughout the Gospels how Jesus was moved to heal hurting people, not with a condescending, pity-laced form of compassion, but rather with a gutsy, earthy, visceral, "get in the mud and muck of life with another person" empathy. Jesus *felt* the pain others were feeling. In our own imperfect way, we too can connect with each other's hurts, and in this protected space, when the time is right, we can also tenderly offer a new vision for someone who has not yet discovered what it means to suffer strong.

As I sat beside a woman's bed where she was lying in horrible pain, she expressed through tears how her debilitating circumstance caused her to feel about herself and God. "It's like we're *cursed*," she cried out. It took me back to so many of my own struggles in trying to make sense of a life I never imagined myself living. It was easy to feel like God had made a mistake—or worse, that He was punishing us. It's a despairing place to be when we feel like no human can fully understand our unique pain—and the God who can understand seems to be part of the problem.

Having been the recipient of some well-intentioned but poorly timed "encouragement" in the past, I'm inclined to offer up my presence and tears before anything else. However, as I sat with this woman in our community, I could not get a certain word out of my head. With some trepidation, I asked if I could pray it over her. With her permission, I spoke to God: "God, take the word *cursed* that hangs like a banner overhead right now and replace it with another *C* word—*chosen*." It was my way of saying, "You feel cursed, crushed, and abandoned, and that's understandable, but we see you as strong, beloved, and chosen. And we will believe in that new identity for you until you can believe it for yourself."

This new name didn't make the woman's pain go away, not by a long shot. And in some ways, it may have made her hurt a bit more for a while as she grappled with the implications. "If I am *chosen*, why would it be for this?" That question is one we all get to lean into at some point in our lives. But as we do, we may eventually begin to ask, "If I am *chosen*, why *not* for this?"

The truth is, we are all invited to suffer strong and to help each other do the same. It's no small task, but it's no small privilege either. Yes, community, like every precious thing, requires much from us. It's easier to talk about the necessary sacrifice of tithing our money, but community is not that different. It requires giving away things we feel entitled to keep.

Our human nature may scream that we've already got our own junk and can't possibly take on someone else's stuff too! Our amygdalas are hardwired to respond with either fight or flight when we encounter suffering. Therefore, the act of compassion takes a certain amount of bravery. In the midst of our own overwhelming hurts, it may be all we can do to not run away from ourselves, let alone someone else. But studies have shown that from a very young age, children's brains can be rewired through experiences of compassion and community to actually shrink their amygdalas and learn to stay instead of running away.

All the more encouraging is that Jesus, the wounded Healer, invites all of us, with His scars and the weight of the world on His shoulders, to take heart. We know the end of the story of suffering in the world. We know it's overcome by a hope that will never die. So we can be present to the pain of others because Jesus is present in ours. He modeled the way of compassion and healing by showing us what it means to say, "Even still, I'm going to stay."

Don't Open Mouth and Insert Foot

At times, we may feel like we've run out of compassion. We've taken on the weight of the hard stories. We've entered into the pain of others for so long. And yet there's a blessed antidote to compassion fatigue—it's more community. As individuals, we can't escape the inevitable hardening of the heart brought on by continued exposure to others' suffering, but our hearts will become soft again for the work ahead if we aren't the only ones holding another's suffering. We are limited as individuals, but in community we transcend those limitations. In the ongoing process of believing a new story about who we are, then forgetting it, and then remembering together, the community that has tracked with us all along can keep helping to mold a new identity in us.

That's not to say we won't make mistakes. Even if we've been through hard things ourselves, we can fall into common traps when we encounter other people in the midst of grief and loss. Seriously, if the words "How are you?" come out of my mouth to someone in pain one more time, I will awkwardly slap myself in the face. It's obvious how they're doing—not great!—so the last thing I need to do is fill the space with dumb questions.

I really like how Sheryl Sandberg offers an easy save when this knee-jerk question does fall out of our mouths. She recommends simply asking, "How are you doing *today*?" Somehow, that simple edit draws the all-encompassing feelings of loss and fear and pain back to the present moment, where they're a little more manageable. It demands no future plans or past excuses. It simply communicates that we're human beings together right now, and you're safe here.

I can't tell you how many well-meaning people tried to offer truth to me when I was in the middle of grieving and how it only made things worse. I haven't been immune to doing the same thing at times, so let me offer some reminders for all of us.

Resist seeing a hurting person's sadness as something to fix; rather, see that person as a human being looking for hope. See them with compassion, like Jesus saw people, and commit to playing your small part in the process of their healing.

Don't quote some Bible verse out of context, just because you don't know what else to say. Don't slap a Jesus sticker on someone's devastated life; they'll need more of Jesus than just a sticker. Instead, lead with a ministry of tears before offering a ministry of truth.

Sit with hurting people. Offer them your presence. Show them you're connecting to their pain. Listen to what they need. Weep with them. It won't make them feel worse; it will make them feel welcomed into communion with you.

Remember that timing is everything. Pay attention. And if you're not sure it's time for truth, then don't give truth yet.

In general, remember less words are the best words. Communicate your truth more with your body than with your mouth. And when the time is right, tell another hurting heart what helped heal yours.

The same woman who felt cursed was lamenting on a different day how misunderstood she felt and how someone's words had hurt her badly. Having also been hurt by insensitive words, I empathized and certainly didn't want to hurt her more with my own words. Yet it seemed she needed to be reminded of a deeper truth than what she was seeing in her wounded state. I told her that the careless words of well-meaning people were always going to be a possibility, but we didn't have to give them the power to hurt us so deeply. I encouraged her to get tougher skin, to keep her heart soft, and to remember just how strong she was becoming through the process.

I immediately felt like a jerk. I'd broken my own rule about not saying too much too soon to someone's hurting heart! I didn't hear from her for a few days and felt kind of sick about it. Just before I was going to reach out, I got a text from her: Thank you for the encouragement. It was just the kind of advice I needed to hear. And you were the only one who could have told it to me so I could actually hear it. Whew, that was a close one! You are loved, I replied.

We may feel that our death-denying brains can't be trusted to handle these kinds of communal situations with the utmost care. We're just too weirded out by it all. But this is no excuse to not enter in. Ecclesiastes 7:2 makes it clear: "It is better to go to a house of mourning than to go to a house of feasting, for death is the destiny of everyone; the living should take this to heart." This act of entering into the "house of mourning" isn't just a charitable act by us toward someone else; rather, it's a vital reminder to ourselves that the dividing lines of life are very thin. One minute, we're the consoler; the next, we're the ones grieving and losing and dying ourselves. Either way, when we go to each other's houses of mourning, we may feel like we're approaching a sketchy haunted house. But walking through a haunted house is much less scary when we hold each other's hands. Leading the way is our compassionate companion, Jesus, so we don't have to be afraid.

Beware Community Imposters

We all need to find our community, but even more, we need to find our soul's board of directors. These are the people whom we choose and who choose us. Amid the noise of other voices around us, these are the ones we can trust. They may not be the people we've known all our lives. They may not be the most pervasive or loudest voices. But they will be the ones we can turn to when we need to remember who we are.

For this reason, we need to be diligent about whom we listen to. Our search for belonging can take us down some dead ends to social groups, including those at church, that appear to be what we're looking for, but really aren't. Maybe you've had this sad experience where it looks like you've found a place to belong but it's actually a thinly disguised framework for narcissism. It looks like we're together sharing needs and resources, but really it's all about *me*, not *we*! Everyone puts on the group name tag and superficial smiles, but the community is actually only a means to getting what the individual wants and needs for himself. "Yes, yes, I'm totally making notes about all your prayer requests in my head, but anyway, back to what I was saying about all *my* stuff!"

Equally as false and painful is the community that functions solely as a tribe, fully embracing of each other as long as everyone looks, thinks, talks, votes, and believes the same. Otherwise, you're out! This kind of tribalism is also thinly disguised narcissism, as it seeks to protect the individual by surrounding her with only mirror images of herself, allowing her to maintain her self-interest free from judgment in an echo chamber designed to look like a genuine community.

Community in its truest sense is about unity, not uniformity. We may find a sense of belonging in certain groups because of what we have in common, but true community is about communion at a much deeper level. It's about sharing our common experience of glorious struggle as humans and helping each other see Jesus throughout our journeys.

This kind of community blurs all the lines and transcends all the labels. It seeks healing for both the individual and the world at the same time. We make God manifest to each other and thus to the world through how we love each other in community. "Jesus loves me" offers us a starting point, but "God so loved the world" is the bigger vision. God's love is personal. We're not anonymous specks of dust. We're seen and known and called to indispensable roles in what God is already doing.

In perfect Southern parlance, Paul tells the church in Corinth, "*All* y'all's bodies are the temple of God" (1 Corinthians 6:19, my paraphrase). That means it's not just *you* as one person trying to make that temple look perfect, but rather all of God's people together building a space for God to dwell among us. Sometimes we may still try to make our own little temple because we think it looks really good and God will like ours best. But next to the communal palace, made by God and all of us, ours looks like an outhouse. Thankfully, God says, "Come, let's build the real thing together."

We're Worth It

God wants us to see ourselves as He sees us—as His beloved child. He acknowledges the worth of each and every human being, and we in turn get to acknowledge that worth in others. As those who are called worthy in God's eyes, we share a God-thread that weaves us together, whether we know it or not, into a tapestry that is bigger and more beautiful than the sum of its parts.

My boys have taught me about this in profound ways. Not long ago, we were in a somewhat seedy downtown area when a man came up to us. This was clearly not his first night on the streets. He wanted to see if we would help him get some dinner. Jay reached for his hand and responded, "We'd love to help you get something to eat. What's your name? Where are you from?" We chatted for a bit with Charles, listening to him tell his hard story and looking him in the eyes.

It seemed like he felt taken care of ever so briefly by this family who had also clearly been through some hard things and who hadn't averted their eyes to pretend he wasn't there. We gave him some money, and he told us he was headed to McDonald's. James, who was ten at the time, spoke up with uncharacteristic boldness. "Can I give you some advice, sir?" We both debated in the next second or two whether to intervene. We'd tried to make the man feel seen and dignified in our small exchange; would our child's advice now make him feel less-than again? "Sir, if you're going to McDonald's, I really recommend the Happy Meal. It's my favorite, and I think you'd really like it." Our minds were blown, and so were our hearts. "I did not see that one coming," I mouthed at Jay as we moved on, beaming with pride that some good things were cooking in our firstborn son.

I guess it shouldn't be a total shocker for James to see people as worthy of love and compassion because he has watched his dad treat people this way his whole life. For eight years, our across-the-street neighbors were a couple with developmental disabilities. They lived independently but with aides who helped them with their daily needs. Apparently, those aides weren't in love with their jobs, or very good at them either, as our neighbor, Janet, would knock on our door multiple times a week, needing help from Jay. I guess she figured I wasn't able to be super helpful, or maybe she just thought Jay was cute, but she never asked me to help, only him.

We had a large anchor door knocker on that house, and no one else we knew actually used that thing except Janet. We might be taking a nap or hanging out in the backyard and be startled by the violent banging of metal against wood twenty times and Janet's not super-subtle shouting: "HELLO! IS ANYBODY HOME? I NEED SOME HELP WITH MY CLOCK!"

She particularly loved to come over right at dinnertime, and every single time she asked for help with the same nonemergency task—resetting one of her clocks to exactly match the time on her cell phone. This required Jay to make a trip across the street to her cat-filled home. Not only are we all highly allergic to cats, but, I'm sorry to say, we're just not crazy about them either. It pains me to admit it, but since we're neither Jesus nor Mother Teresa, there were a few dinnertimes when we'd just sat down at the table only to hear Janet at our door, and instead of jumping up, we just tried to stay very quiet. She'd eventually stop banging and go home. But nine times out of ten, Jay would get up from the table with a little smile at the humor of the situation and go help Janet know what time it really was.

When we see another person as an inherently valuable reflection of God, we naturally honor their needs. We don't dismiss their requests for our help as beneath us, because all those requests—the weird and the wonderful—are worthy. God wants us to see Him in the same way; unlike the Wolfs, God doesn't hide out when we come knocking. Rather, He's already on the front porch smiling, welcoming us with His hands outstretched and saying, "I'd love to help you fix your clock."

A New Covenant

The prophet Jeremiah spoke of a time long ago when God changed the rules for the people He loved. Rather than holding them to a strict set of laws they had tried, and failed, to follow through generations, He made a new covenant with them. He would inscribe His laws on their hearts and, in so doing, bind them to Him in a way that would last forever (Jeremiah 31). In the same way, healing in community is based on a covenant—a commitment to be there for one another, no matter what life places on our path.

Several years after the stroke, my neurosurgeon, Dr. Gonzalez, discovered an aneurysm on the "good side" of my brain, totally separate from the AVM and four aneurysms that caused my initial stroke. We confidently signed up for him to perform the removal surgery, but the morning beforehand, I felt overwhelmed with anxiety, deeply fearful that I would certainly die on the table. Through a series of encounters with people who reminded me that my soul was anchored to something that could transcend any storm, I was propelled from my fearful isolation into a comforting community. When we went to church that morning, a huge group surrounded me in prayer. As they prayed, we cried together for the history of hurts we shared. They anointed me with oil, an ancient tradition and a reminder that I was set apart by a loving God for His purposes.

In recognition of that simple, life-giving act, at Hope Heals Camp we anoint each other with oil. After our final dinner together, both those with and without physical disabilities get doused in acknowledgment that though we may feel displaced in this world, we are displaced *together*, set apart with God and for God and for each other. We get our oil from a place in Tennessee called Thistle Farms, where it's made by a collective of women who've been freed from sex trafficking, addiction, and abuse. Our wild and wonderful time of anointing honors the sweet by-products that come from lives that have been hard pressed but not crushed. It's not a cure but a covenant. It's not about erasing the hurts but about remembering the hope.

Shortly before His death, Jesus was anointed with oil by a woman whose life He had changed (John 12:1–8). I imagine He was still smelling its sweet scent as He endured all manner of pain and suffering. Today, as we literally and figuratively offer the oil of our lives to each other, the fragrance carries us through whatever pain lies ahead, knowing that while we may suffer, we'll never suffer alone.

Recreating Community

We recently moved from California back to Georgia to be closer to our families. We'd both grown up in the South but had called Los Angeles home for nearly fourteen years. We've been asked repeatedly throughout our transition to this new season how we feel about being back in our community, as if the essence of community is ultimately rooted in one's history and proximity. Surely, many have assumed, a place as self-focused and anonymous as LA would not foster living life together.

Ironically, it took moving to such a place to truly understand what community is meant to be. In a city of mostly transplanted dreamers, we had the opportunity to create a different kind of community—one not fixed to history or tribe or self, but one where true communion was found, not just in spite of our differences, but because of them. When we rolled up to a church that offered us a home, we offered it ourselves in return. The investment of our lives and the connections we made in that community changed us and our story forever.

As we moved into a new chapter in Atlanta, we longed to find a community to do life with again—and we have. It formed, once again, in the only place we've found the kind of community that makes the invisible God visible—*the church*. In a beautifully full-circle experience, after being deeply ministered to by pastor Louie Giglio and his wife, Shelley, we now call Passion City Church our church home. I once joked onstage that their marketing team made a great choice in calling it that instead of Suffering City Church. I mean, who would put *suffering* on the front of anything? Well, ahem, maybe us . . . see the front cover of this book. But it's not usually super appealing, is it, to humans who prefer to avoid their own suffering, much less take on someone else's too? We don't normally like to connect our ideas of healing, passion, and compassion with the fact that all of this requires *suffering together*.

Passion for anything means loving it enough to sacrifice for it. And this is the picture of what happens when, against all natural impulses and excuses, we share the burden of someone else's suffering. In so doing, their load is undeniably lightened, but our load is surprisingly lightened too. In this experience of staying and sharing the struggle, we release a bit more of the burden of our own selves, and we receive healing for our wounds that can only be found in that place.

Our new community has embraced us with overwhelming love, as if we've been here all along. As we've settled into this new city and season, we're humbled to know people inside and outside the church, people in our neighborhood and kids' schools, and even a digital community spread far and wide that has followed us throughout our story. God has brought us together, and we're so grateful. We've learned some things about how we best work in community, what we need, where our boundaries lie and where they should lie; but mostly we've learned just how desperately we *need* true communion to continue living out our unique calling and to understand ourselves, other people, and God.

In the years since our lives changed forever, we've met friends in real life and online whose stories of tragedy are different from ours but whose responses have been the same. Like us, they're trying to find themselves and God in the midst of their pain. It seemed appropriate for us to create a club, a very exclusive club, with the simple but very costly requirement that one must have been through life's worst and come out seeing its best. Everywhere we go, we meet new members and invite them to join our Young Suffering Club. It's a club no one would seek out, but once they're in, they may never want to leave. And you—new friend, fellow sufferer, young (or not so young)—are invited to join too. We're working on an official clubhouse. Maybe one day we'll meet up on this journey and build it together.

CHAPTER 10

GLORIOUS SCARS

Redefining Healing

Jay

In the wee hours of the morning, just a few days after Katherine's stroke, I sat in disbelief by her ICU bed. It was dark, save for the blinking lights of the machine cityscape that surrounded her. It was quiet, save for the sickening whoosh of the ventilator and the rise and fall of her chest with each artificial breath. I was unable to think or sleep, haunted by the memory of her calling my name for the last time before the ambulance took her away, anguished by the horrifying acts done to her body and brain during a sixteen-hour-long surgery, and shocked by the nightmarish sight in front of me. Katherine, my love, the mother of my child, was propped up, swollen and unrecognizable, with bloodied hair, bruised face, and half-shaved, bandaged head. She had always embodied confidence, strength, and beauty. Now I could hardly look at her without wanting to sob uncontrollably. I sensed deeply that God hadn't spared her life only to leave her to die in this place, but having to endure the present circumstances felt nearly as terrible as death.

I began reading through the book of Job, because where else do you turn in the Bible when you want to know you're not the only one in the world who's gone through some horrible thing? The theme of God's overwhelming care for His people, hand in hand with His overwhelming otherness from us, came through strongly. Of course, this was both comforting and alarming. Is this the God I always thought I knew?

In the midst of Job's suffering, his friends tried to comfort him, and though their diatribes were not exactly what I'd recommend saying to anyone in the midst of acute suffering (remember, less words are the best words), a phrase I'd never noticed before sprang from the page in Job 5:18: "For he wounds, but he also binds up; he injures, but his hands also heal."

This concept was hard for me to process. It seemed so contrary to how I thought God worked. Only a broken world wounds. Only evil injures. Yet here I sat in front of a woman who'd been wounded and injured in order that she might be healed. When I looked at her neurosurgeon, Dr. Gonzalez, I didn't think of him as her wounder; rather, I saw him as her lifesaver, her healer. He'd intentionally sacrificed and even destroyed parts of her brain and body for the greater purpose of sparing her life. Wounding Katherine was not the doctor's end goal, but the wounding was necessary if he hoped to save her. And so it is with God, except He knows the outcome. He never wounds us more deeply than He can heal us.

Of course, we couldn't see that then. It would take years to gain a perspective that gave meaning to our horrendous experience. And pondering the ministry of Jesus didn't exactly make our under-standing of healing much clearer. Jesus healed the sick, disabled, demon-possessed, and even dead. Sometimes it was because of the faith of the person; other times He was simply moved by compas-sion for them without regard to their faith. Sometimes it was like He set up a booth and healed droves of people in one sitting; other times He healed just one person, leaving all the others not healed, and then slipped out the back. Is there any rhyme or reason to this? Are there lessons to be learned or a formula to memorize? At the end of the day, there seems to be a pattern: healing is in God's control, but we are invited into the process.

It's human nature to want a cause-and-effect explanation for suffering. We want to know what to do to prevent it from hap-pening to us. We want to know which sins are okay and which will result in us being struck blind or losing the house or the child. We want to know how to get God's attention when we're suffer-ing. *Please, God, just tell me how You want me to pray. Just tell me the right words. I'll say them so many times—shout them from the rooftops even—if You'll just let me off the hook, if You'll just restore what I've lost.* Prayers and confession are good, but if we use them to try to control outcomes, then we're missing the point that God is God and we are not.

John 5 tells the story of Jesus encountering a man who had suffered for decades living in a body that didn't work and in a society that didn't even see him as a human being. "Do you want to be healed?" Jesus asked him. Surely a resounding *yes* would be expected. Yet the man didn't answer with a straightforward "Duh!"; rather, he explained why he hadn't been healed, how others had taken all the healing that could have been his, how no one would help him.

Jesus already knew the man's history. He already knew the man's heart. Jesus didn't ask him if he believed. Jesus didn't commend his faith. Jesus simply had compassion on him and gave him the healing that had been out of reach his whole life. Then He gave him a new identity. To paraphrase, "You have been healed in body and soul. You were a victim. You were alone. You were imprisoned in your body and in your sin. Now, because of this healing, you are an overcomer, and you will never be alone. You are free. Now go live differently."

But why did Jesus choose to heal this particular man? Did Jesus just feel sorry for him? Was it the start of some grand domino effect that would change the world? I don't know. I do know we're still talking about this story thousands of years later. This man's painful life gives us a picture of how we all long to be healed yet place obstacles between us and whatever kind of healing God chooses for us. We don't want to be vulnerable, to feel the powerlessness of perhaps not getting the outcome we desire. We've waited too long for the miracle that has never happened, and our hearts can't take any more exposure. We've felt alone, and now we're too weary in body and soul to take even one more step forward. And yet there was grace for this social outcast, and there is grace for us too.

Admittedly, even the overcoming of such obstacles and acceptance of Jesus' invitation to healing will lead us into more mystery than clarity here and now, but we'll never be at peace until we're at peace with this. This perspective on our smallness in the grander scheme of things can make us feel insignificant and unseen, or it can make us feel worthy and extravagantly loved, chosen out of a crowd of hurts, and given a chance to get up and walk and live again.

Another moment in the gospel of John gives us a clue about the heart of God in the midst of our pain. Jesus saw a man who had been blind his whole life. He had no doubt been living in physical and relational and spiritual darkness. He was known by his community but left to beg on the street. Jesus *saw* him when no one else did.

The disciples, kind of like medical students barreling into some poor patient's hospital room, began analyzing the situation. "Hmm, whose fault is this? So sad. Do you think he sinned and got punished for it by being struck blind? Bless his heart. Wait, maybe it was his parents' sin. Sins of the father are the worst." Jesus may well have given His friends the stink eye, communicating clearly that although the man was blind, he wasn't deaf!

Jesus saw a man who had never even seen himself, and in that moment, Jesus spoke words that have healed broken hearts for thousands of years, that have given purpose to every manner of pain: "This happened so that the works of God might be displayed in him" (John 9:3).

Our son John (whose name means, "the Lord has been gracious") was named for the gospel writer, and this verse from that writer is our anchoring prayer over his life. In places of darkness and weakness, in places where John can't even see himself, we pray that God's glory will shine the brightest.

Glorious Scars

To this day, Katherine bears many scars from all the wounds that saved her life and brought her healing. Some are quite visible, like the trach scar centered just above her collarbones. Others are less visible, like her oldest and most impressive one, which runs from the top of her backbone to the base of her skull. It looks like railroad tracks up her neck and through her hair, from where her bleeding brain was exposed during the lifesaving surgery. "Scars mean you lived," Katherine always says matter-of-factly. We never considered having them "fixed," but we did live in LA after all. I'm sure we could have covered up those reminders of the wounding. But in so doing, we would have covered up the reminders of the healing too.

In his letter to the Corinthians, Paul, who was afflicted with his own persistent disability—maybe even vision problems—and tremendous lifelong suffering of all kinds, declared that God's works aren't displayed only in the fruition of a hoped-for outcome—healing of the weakness or pain—but rather that God's works and His power are most evident in the weakness itself: "My [Jesus'] grace is sufficient for you, for my power is made perfect in weakness" (2 Corinthians 12:9).

If our weakness is not entirely apparent, then God's strength will not be entirely apparent either. God's works are powerfully evident in His healing of our hurts, but perhaps even more profoundly in the not-yet healing. That's why *how* we suffer matters. Suffering strong offers a unique testimony to all who witness it, unveiling an "in the midst of" God who is too big and too good not to be worshiped, whether or not our longed-for outcome materializes.

"God allows what He hates to accomplish what He loves," says our dear friend Joni Eareckson Tada, a woman who has lived with quadriplegia since a diving accident more than fifty years ago. Those words have brought healing to our hearts, yet to some this proclamation may come across as painfully disorienting. *Why would God allow awful things? Why would He wound us? Doesn't that mean He's somehow complicit in our suffering? That He wants us to suffer?* I guess it would if God were bound by our understanding of complicity, by our cause-and-effect logic, by the confines of the story we can see; but He is not. Yes, He allows kids to be born blind and young women to nearly die and all kinds of horrible things to happen. But these wounds have His glory all over them. Our sufferings display His works unlike anything else in our humanity. And unlike us, whose vision is so limited, God sees a bigger-picture love coming behind our suffering, through it and all around it. While pain may be all we can see right now, in the not-too-distant future we'll see only love.

Quite beautifully, scars can also lead to deep communion between fellow sufferers. For us, a trach scar sighting on a stranger in the grocery store may as well be a neon sign over their head. Katherine, especially, never misses a chance to say hello. *I see you. What's your story? I'm so sorry. Here's my story. Me too.* Scars are visible reminders of an invisible grace, and we can be those reminders for each other.

At a retreat called Seasons Weekend, we ended our time of intensely healing reflection by making small pieces of pottery that represented the bond we experienced in suffering together and in suffering with a God who suffers too. It was a profoundly meaningful exercise. I will never forget how one friend's would-be pottery "cup of suffering" unmistakably resembled a hard taco shell. She may have felt slightly shamed at the group's unanimous and uncontrollable laughter over her art. If she had dreams of being a ceramicist, we may have shut those down. But we lovingly reminded her that she'd never have to eat that taco full of suffering alone. And then we all died laughing again. It was good medicine—healing in every way.

Jesus invited His disciples into an even more amazing encounter with Him. When He appeared to His friends after His death, He had resurrected into a never-going-to-die version of Himself. Yet there was a startling detail to that version, a detail no one would have thought of as perfect. His resurrected body still bore those horrible scars, those terrible reminders of what had happened to Him at the end. Were the scars only there so His disciples would recognize Him? Is He the only one with scars in heaven? I guess we'll see one day, but for now, that image reminds us that one of the final pictures Jesus left us of Himself *included the scars* that healed the world. Love is His end goal, but sacrifice and scars are the means to that end.

Any human with a heart, especially one that's been broken, longs for healing—healing for themselves and healing for the world. Yet our individual paths to healing, like the paths to every priceless thing, can be as varied as the human hearts seeking it. A friend lovingly pointed out that the scar on Katherine's knee where a metal rod was inserted after she badly broke her leg is in the shape of an anchor, the ancient symbol of hope and the symbol that brands our ministry, Hope Heals. Our scars tell stories, whether we want to hear them or not. More than tattoos, which we get to choose to tell a story on our bodies, scars are the story we receive about the life we're still living. We've all got scars, if nowhere else than on our hearts. When we reveal our scars to ourselves and to others, they act as a sort of sacrament, which is to say they are an outward symbol of an inner experience. They are Ebenezers of just how far God has brought us and thus how far He will take us. They mean we lived. Now we have to figure out what we are living for.

The Ultimate Healing

As we've walked this journey, Katherine and I have come to believe that the *process* of healing is in fact the healing. When we ask God to heal us in the one way we think of healing, He says, "You're setting the bar too low; let Me heal your soul."

One night recently, I watched Katherine from backstage as she shared her story. I blinked back tears at the stories I'd heard dozens of times before because she told them with such tenderness, like it was the very first telling. Her tears flowed freely as she preached truth to her own wounded heart. As hope flowed into Katherine and overflowed from her onto every person in that place, including me, she proclaimed with authority and gratitude, "As I sit in this wheelchair with a paralyzed face and messed-up voice and a body that doesn't work, it may not look like I'm healed to you. But hear me now, I have been healed where it matters the most—in my broken heart and soul." Mic drop—except I think she just kept on preaching for another thirty minutes because, well, she had so many more good things to say, and also, I wasn't onstage to perform my time-tested, subtle tap on her back when her time was up.

After she finished, there was a standing ovation and more tears all around. I hugged her and told her I was so proud to call her my wife. I helped her get set up to meet the crowd in the atrium. Getting to hug and laugh and cry with people, hearing their stories and thinking through their hard questions, is as important as, if not more important than, anything said onstage. We call it a "holy but heavy" time, because it is. Vulnerability in community is transformational, but it can also leave you, well, vulnerable, and sometimes that exposure can hurt.

About a half hour into our interaction with the crowd, we heard the words we'd heard many times in similar places over the years—words that always put a pit in our stomachs: "Can I pray for your healing?" Katherine—slightly taken aback given the pretty straightforward proclamation she had just delivered regarding her healing—still graciously invited this woman toward her. Simultaneously, I had to muffle my scream for "SECURITY!" Then Katherine gave me her own time-tested, subtle tap on my back, and I knew she was okay. Katherine has a loving response to this type of well-intended offer. She'll say, "Of course you can pray for my physical healing—thank you so much—but can you also pray for my gossipy mouth or my negative spirit of judgment and comparison or for my marriage and kids? We'll take all the healing prayer we can get!"

Tonight, however, before those words could come out of

Katherine's mouth, the woman placed her hand on the paralyzed side of Katherine's face and began going for it, hard. Unfortunately, it seemed the would-be healer had also gone for the deep-dish pizza that night and had neglected to thoroughly wash her hands afterward. Not only is Katherine's face numb on the right side, but she is also stone-cold deaf in her right ear, so she had to keep squinting open her eyes to tell if the woman had finished. Several minutes later, the woman finally had said all the faith-filled words she could think of, and she released Katherine from her sweaty grip. The woman then hunkered down, eye to eye with Katherine, searching for new symmetry, her eyes probing every imperfection like a Beverly Hills plastic surgeon. "Does it feel any different?" the woman asked. "Well," Katherine said kindly, "I don't have any feeling on that side, but maybe it just takes a few minutes to work? I'll let you know!"

Man looks at the outward appearance, but God looks at the heart. Though this woman may have missed that verse (1 Samuel 16:7), we tried to remember it as we looked at her heart. She was longing for healing for Katherine in the ways that made the most sense to her, in the ways she could see. Ironically, her search for healing had done just a little bit of wounding too. Not only had she taken away some of Katherine's dignity (maybe just ask before you go touching someone else's face with your less-than-pristine, Hot Pocket hands), but she had taken away some of Katherine's agency too. Katherine had claimed words about her own identity as someone already healed by God, yet this woman effectively said to her, "No, you're not."

We found ourselves in a similar setting not long ago when a

man asked us a totally different question, which hurt our hearts for a totally different reason. This man was tall and lumbering, probably in his sixties. He was an imposing figure, made even more so as he walked with a limp and a cane. His face was paralyzed and scraped along the side, likely from a fall. He told us how a worsening condition in his brain had taken away so many parts of his life he had always taken for granted. His marriage had broken up along with his body and heart. He gripped our book in his working hand, and with tears streaming down and a voice slurred by his injury, he said our story of healing had played a vital role in his own healing. And yet, with the tender longing of someone who has tasted all of life's bittersweetness, he asked, "But when do you know it's finally time to stop believing for a miracle? When should I stop asking God to heal me?"

Swallowing a burning lump in my throat, I grabbed this man's arm as Katherine grabbed his hand, tears of understanding in both our eyes. She said, "You are a miracle, friend. We are all miracles here together. And the world needs to hear from more wounded healers like us. Don't ever stop believing that God will heal you at just the right time and in every way you need and in more ways than you could ever imagine."

Who doesn't want a fast-forward outcome sometimes? Who doesn't want to just arrive at the promised ending *right now*? But a life in fast-forward is no way to experience the grandeur of a story. A life is best lived in real time. Otherwise, we'll never be able to pay attention to what God is doing in us and, moreover, who God is becoming to us.

After a decade of living with scars, both obvious and not

so obvious, Katherine and I continue to say and believe with the deepest assurance that *Katherine is healed*. Naturally, in the beginning we longed to know what we needed to do to help make physical healing happen for her. We all wanted her near-death experience to be a blip on the timeline of her life. Instead, it would be the story of second-chance grace for the rest of her life and for lots of other lives too. If she'd left the hospital unscathed, we would have celebrated the miracle in awe and wonder. We would have worshiped a God who could do something so extraordinary. And then we would have gone back to our lives, still in the afterglow. After reentering the story we were living before, the most terrible thing likely would have happened—we eventually would have forgotten. It's inevitable that even the most powerful miracle experiences fade over time. Humans have been forgetting miracles, and thus forgetting God, since the beginning. And more than just forgetting the miracle, we would have missed out on a healing that is truer and deeper than we ever knew we needed.

Does that mean it wouldn't be amazingly sweet to take a jog with Katherine, like we did on our first "date"? Wouldn't it be fun to see her driving our kids to soccer practice (though she insists the roads are safer without her behind the wheel)? Wouldn't it be incredible to watch her easily cook and eat all the foods she ever wanted without coughing or choking on them? Wouldn't it be stunning to witness God wipe away every scar and blemish and paralysis and pain from her head to her toes? Of course the answer to all those things is *yes*. And we don't put God in a box. (No one should, because I don't think God likes it in there.) We don't ever stop believing that God can heal Katherine in any and every way possible. Yet during this process of longing for healing and witnessing healing and giving thanks for healing, great and small, we find ourselves less desiring what used to be and more mindful of the miracle that is.

About a year after the stroke, a friend who had struggled with infertility shared a Bible passage that had comforted her deeply. Habakkuk 3:17–18 reads:

> Though the fig tree does not bud
>> and there are no grapes on the vines,
> though the olive crop fails
>> and the fields produce no food,
> though there are no sheep in the pen
>> and no cattle in the stalls,
> yet I will rejoice in the LORD,
>> I will be joyful in God my Savior.

As the friend had done, Katherine was inspired to rewrite this verse for our story. "Though I cannot walk, and I am confined to a wheelchair, though half my face is paralyzed and I cannot even smile, though I am extremely impaired and cannot take care of my own baby boy, yet I will rejoice in the Lord. I will be joyful in God my Savior." This was her act of joyful rebellion. She was acknowledging the reality of her situation and the depth of her loss, but she was also declaring that those things would not stop her from worship.

Even when we have no fruit on the withered vines of our lives and feel to our core that we'll never have any fruit again, our suffering can produce a harvest in our lives like none we've seen before. Our friend Nicole traveled to the Bordeaux region of France, where she visited exclusive vineyards and simple monasteries, all practicing the ancient tradition of winemaking. The amount of effort and tender care required to summon food from the earth can be astounding, and this is certainly true of grapes.

It is said that the story of the year the grapes were harvested can be told in the glass of wine produced. And more than that, if there was a drought or harsh temperatures that year, if the vine struggled mightily to live amid all the elements arrayed against it during that "difficult vintage," as they call it, then the fruit of that struggle is believed to be particularly special grapes. And then those grapes are turned into particularly special and delicious wine. If the struggle doesn't kill the vine, it instills the vine with something better than it contained before. When Nicole gifted us with a bottle of wine from 2008—the year of Katherine's stroke—she said with a smile, "It was a particularly difficult vintage, but the fruit from it is especially sweet."

Katherine and I have had a paradigm shift in our understanding of healing because we've tasted this sweetness. We're being filled up by God in a way that feels as though it lacks for nothing. We understand now that healing and wholeness are not the same thing. It may just be semantics; one person's healing is another person's wholeness. *I am now healed; I am now whole.* These terms are used interchangeably at times, but in this process of seeking strength on the other side of our wounds, it has been necessary to make a distinction. Our expectations will always be the place of our making or breaking. We may very well be experiencing healing and still not *feel* healed like we thought we would. We may be overlooking present healing in a search for future wholeness. Do we expect to find total healing on this earth for all our wounds? If we do, then we'll be sorely disappointed. It's no major news flash that the bodies and world we live in are not safe; our circumstances are unknown, and the very laws of nature in and around us are moment by moment causing us and everything else to fall apart. How then can we ever fully experience, right now, the total healing we wish for? We can't.

A line from Wendell Berry's poem "Marriage" describes this dichotomy. "We hurt, and are hurt, and have each other for healing. It is healing. It is never whole."[22] Our marriages and relationships are great sources of healing, even and especially when they are also great sources of our hurting. However, they were never intended to, nor could they ever, make us whole. Only God can do that. And one day with Him, face-to-face, we *will* be whole, more so than we ever knew was possible. But it is not yet. That ache in our healed but still hurting hearts is a reminder that there is *more*, that we ought not to stop in the middle, disillusioned and disappointed. The healing we experience this side of heaven is but the seed of wholeness that will one day bloom into something altogether different and deeper . . . and it will be glorious.

CHAPTER 11

THE PATH BEFORE US

Redefining Calling

Katherine

"Wow, ladies and gentlemen, what a huge honor it is to be with you today," I said, beaming. My palms were sweaty, but my voice was strong. This was a really big and important crowd. "My name is Katherine, and I wanted to thank you for joining me in the fight against injustice and inequality. As Dr. Martin Luther King Jr. said, 'Darkness cannot drive out darkness; only light can do that. Hate cannot drive out hate; only love can do that.'[23] God brings light, and God is love, so we need God to help us in the fight against darkness and hate. Look to your right and look to your left. This world is missing something valuable if any of you is not fully able to use all of your talents and gifts. Let's help lift each other up, not bring each other down! We can do it together. Thank you so much." I smiled big and gave a little curtsy.

"Katherine, dinner's ready!" my mom yelled from downstairs.

"Okay, everybody, I've gotta take five, but I'll be back in just a little bit with a very powerful story about hope from Anne Frank. Don't go anywhere!" I shut the door behind me as I ran out of my room. The auditorium of dolls and stuffed animals didn't move a muscle. I just knew they couldn't wait to hear more. And they would.

I was ten years old and admittedly a bit of a weird kid, now that I think about it. My closet contained a permanent audience ready for any impromptu performance, motivational speech, or sermon. I'm proud to say all the American Girl dolls came to accept Jesus. The Madame Alexanders were a little iffier, but I think many good seeds were planted. Interestingly, at that time of my life, I also couldn't get enough of the stories from the civil rights movement and the Holocaust, which swirled in my head and heart constantly. It was kind of sweet, considering I was a white girl in the South (I guess I still am that), but I knew even then that we needed to seek out and tell each other stories of hope in the midst of great struggle, so I did to whoever would listen.

I would later go on to a natural career in theatre, including a triumphant moment in the one-act play in high school where my skirt fell off during my monologue (thank goodness for petticoats), and I went with it as though it was part of the script. This performance earned me the "Best Actress in the State of Georgia" title. Then came the study of communications and Christian women's leadership in college, followed by the move to Los Angeles and further pursuit of this funny thing I'd always done—public speaking, often in front of a camera. I felt like I was born for it.

At the same time, I had the opportunity to provide life-giving leadership for one of our church's most flourishing groups, the Young Marrieds. Then in an instant, all the life, identity, dreams, and hope I'd known crashed down around me. I was left with a grim prognosis, life-altering disabilities, a painful recovery, and an unknown future. But over time, new life and different dreams came roaring back. Though the calling I had to public speaking was amplified, it was actually the same calling it had always been. God was calling me to become who I already was, who He'd been calling me to become all along, even in my new circumstances.

"Have you ever felt like you were supposed to do something really big with your life?" eleven-year-old James asked me as we tucked him into bed recently. He'd just finished watching some superhero show, no doubt. He also has a small penchant for the dramatic, like his mama, but he asked the question so earnestly that I couldn't help but smile with recognition. "Yeah, I've totally felt that way too. And, son, there are big things ahead for you and for everyone who lets God use them. Thankfully, we don't have to save the world—that job is way bigger than just us—but we get to be part of what God is already doing in the world, and that's no small thing."

James may have already been asleep before my sermonette was over. I guess he's almost like a new life-size doll I get to give speeches to, except he can talk back and walk away, which is not as ideal. However, he does remind me of myself in so many ways and of all people who are seeking a big life and a big God. We may not fully grasp just how fleeting and fragile our existence is, but we know deep down that we want our lives to matter. Sometimes, though, how that will look feels elusive. Maybe we have too many options, or seemingly none at all. Maybe our talents point one way, and our opportunities another.

It's natural to look to our passions and dreams for answers to the question of calling, but a calling from God is deeper than our desires for ourselves. If dreams reflect an inner longing, callings reflect an outer need. Callings are heard within us but start outside us. Our dreams may change, and they probably should change as we mature, but that doesn't mean God's calling on our lives changes. He's calling each of us to be who He always created us to be. His beloved child. A witness to the light in the darkness. A vessel overflowing with hope.

Jay and I had sat down to lunch with a couple I didn't know well but who had long pastored a church near the college where we met. After we'd spoken at their church that Sunday morning, the woman said matter-of-factly, "I've been praying for you since the day of your stroke, but I had no idea that I wasn't actually praying for your physical recovery." I had to put down my cup of coffee for this one. "Thanks, I think?" I replied, a little confused. "Today I realized that all this time I was praying for you, I was actually praying for a new ministry to begin."

Another friend in LA, the embodiment of a no-nonsense Texas-bred woman, was reported to have said after my stroke, "Well, who else could this have happened to but Katherine?" Again, "Thanks, I think?" But what she was getting at was a vision she had of God's calling for my life. Not that I was called to nearly die, but that I was called to survive and suffer and live in a unique way. This was something she could attest to, as she had known me before everything changed, and she saw parts of me that would be strangely and perfectly, fearfully and wonderfully, suited to this unexpected new chapter in my story.

I cried out to God early on in my disability, "I want to tell people about You—I always have—but I don't want to be the miracle girl in the wheelchair doing it. This isn't the life I imagined when I told my dolls to never give up hope." But then I met other people in wheelchairs and their parents or spouses or siblings or kids, none of whom had ever pictured this life for themselves or their families when they were little either. Then it became clearer. These were my people. This was my calling. This chair wasn't an obstacle to my calling, but it was a greater unveiling of my calling. In fact, it had become my seat of honor.

As our pastor, Louie Giglio, has said, "Pain is a platform." It's not that no one wanted to hear what I thought about overcoming struggle before my stroke—in my privileged, had-it-all-together state. I did have a very attentive doll audience, after all. This isn't to say that one's voice only truly inspires after they've had a massive trauma—please don't go making up or subjecting yourself to more suffering than will inevitably come without your help—but it is to say that the world needs more true and vulnerable stories of loss and struggle woven through with healing and hope. And as our former pastor, Drew Sams, has said, people of hope get to "renarrate the world." That's because we have a special lens through which we see the world and thus through which we see suffering. We're charged with telling the story of God in the world to the world.

It has become my calling to tell everyone in wheelchairs, physical or invisible ones, that God promises to pour His goodness into their hard lives and broken hearts. He offers freedom, not in spite of their constraints, but in the midst of them. He has plans to heal their suffering with His undying strength. These were so many of the same ideas I had in my heart from the start, but now it wasn't just my words that preached; it was my life. It wasn't just a book I'd read; it was my story too. God had taken my misery and given me a ministry. He had cleaned up my mess and left me with a message.

Called to Perseverance

For nearly ten years after my stroke, I got around being pushed in a cheap, manual wheelchair. I've got nothing against those. I thought it was great! The airlines treated it like the discus in a discus throw, but no matter. It did the trick. There was, however, one slight issue. The wheels didn't exactly turn on a dime. They were more like a grocery cart than a finely tuned machine. And if I were left to my own devices, "propelling" myself along with my feet (my right hand doesn't have fine motor control, so I couldn't wheel with my hands), I would quickly find that the most effective option was to just stay straight. Trying to turn right or left was clunky and slow.

One day very early on after the stroke, Jay and I were leaving a hotel pool after visiting some friends who were staying there. I even had on a swimsuit, though my feeding tube prevented me from actually getting in the water. We were feeling confident and a little more normal. Our car was parked on the street, and we needed to venture off the sidewalk across some thick grass. To make it a shorter distance for me to walk, Jay pushed the chair onto the grass.

What happened next made a woman dancing next to the hot tub literally drop her bottle of champagne and fall into the bushes with a scream. The wheels of the chair got caught in the grass and immediately stopped moving while my weak little body kept moving forward. It was the first and last time I fell out of the chair with Jay on duty. Naturally, my swimsuit cover got dramatically ripped off, and I rolled like a stuntwoman into some dog poop. It was nothing if not an inappropriate entry to *America's Funniest Home Videos*. Jay was mortified, but I was fine.

Perhaps it's not so different with our callings. There's a path that may not be easy, but it's one laid out just for us. The author of Hebrews charges us to run our race with perseverance (Hebrews 12:1–2). Fortunately, God is not asking us to blaze our own trail. He's inviting us to stay on the path and get into the groove of what He's already doing. This call to perseverance means the race will be longer than we think. It means the race will be so hard at times that we may be tempted to quit or change course.

Yet this call to perseverance also means there's an end in sight. Fixing our eyes on the finish line, on Jesus, both focuses and motivates us. We don't have to waste energy calculating who is farther along in the race than us or whose race looks easier or better than ours. We won't be able to gauge our progress based on others now, but in this kind of race, focusing on the finish is all we need to fuel our perseverance. If Jesus has called us to it, then He will call us through it.

To mix the metaphor a bit, it's so easy to wonder why our own grass looks so dead compared to everyone else's luscious green lawns. Our California front yard spent many seasons looking like a prison yard. This was because the shade of two huge trees blocked all the sunlight, but it also may have had something to do with us forgetting to water our yard. When our kids ran around in the dry summer, it looked like something out of the Dust Bowl during the Great Depression. In contrast, our neighbor's yard was bright green and inviting. Their sprinklers gave the fountains of Las Vegas a run for their money. It was glorious. Come to think of it, though, there was also a drought in California, so it was probably illegal, but I guess they were willing to risk it for that carpet of green. I think we had a sprinkler, but it must have broken, and then we must have forgotten to fix it. Maybe we just thought it was automatically watering while we were asleep.

Perhaps we should have spent more time becoming students of our own yard, the space we had been given. Maybe we should have looked more into watering our yard and fixing our sprinklers rather than spending time just wishing our yard was green like someone's else. Their grass was greener than ours because they were actually watering it.

We each have something unique to offer the world. We are called to spend more time tending what God has given us and less time craning our necks at our neighbors. Paul wrote to the Galatians, "Make a careful exploration of who you are and the work you have been given, and then sink yourself into that. Don't be impressed with yourself. Don't compare yourself with others. Each of you must take responsibility for doing the creative best you can with your own life" (Galatians 6:4–5 MSG). In our search for calling, the best place to look is right in front of us. As we've discussed, limitations don't have to be losses; they can be the avenues to our flourishing.

This is particularly true if we stay focused and creative within their boundaries, if we care for and cherish what's inside them. I cry every time I think of this quote Jay wrote at the end of our book *Hope Heals*: "One day, we will see. One day, the arc of our stories will all make perfect sense. One day, we will trace the lines of our scars and find them to have fallen in the most pleasant of places, to see in them our great inheritance. One day, we won't need to hope, nor will we need to be healed because we will be face-to-face with the source of both, the source of everything . . . Jesus."[24] Nothing to add there, right?

I suppose if "building your house on the rock instead of on sand" is a fitting enough metaphor for our wedding and marriage, then lot lines must be a great metaphor for our assignments in life. Numbers 33 introduces this idea with the instruction that when God's people entered the land they had long awaited, the Promised Land, they were each to be given a lot. Some would be big, and some would be small, and the size would have nothing to do with anything they could control. Yet the lots would be their very own piece of God's promise for them to live and love and flourish on. We've all been given a lot in life—it's our assignment. And we've all been given *a lot* in life—it's our abundance.

In Psalm 16:6, David sings the praise of his personal property survey: "The boundary lines have fallen for me in pleasant places; surely I have a delightful inheritance." David is not posting these words next to a picture of an over-the-top mansion with an even more over-the-top car parked in front of it, with an over-the-top diamond-draped supermodel sitting nonchalantly on the hood in an appropriately over-the-top evening gown, with the caption "Today's office view" and the hashtag #blessed. No, David's lot was a bit more rustic for sure, but so much more valuable and a whole heck of a lot more #BLESSED.

This psalm likely was written during a time of great trouble for David, as it opens with a straightforward "keep me safe, my God." David is acknowledging that through his struggles against his enemies and betrayals by his friends, he had been called into a unique lot by God and for God and with God. The same God who had given him victory over Goliath and an anointing as king had also given him this lot, so he could trust that it was good. Yet David's lot would eventually also include adultery, murder, shame, rebellious children, incestuous children, rape, more murder, conspiracy, and loss. (And I thought a wheelchair and some garden variety dysfunction in my own lot was a bummer!)

Though David probably didn't see all that coming when he described his lot as a *pleasant* place, the same word is used later in the psalm to describe the pleasures found only in close proximity to God (verse 11). I can only imagine that when this deeply flawed man after God's own heart found his lot filled with such great pain, he also found it filled with a deeper experience of those pleasures in God. Embracing the lot we've been given is about embracing the God who gives it. So no matter what it's filled with, we're already filled by Him. Our experience of purpose in life is not based on the size of the gift but on the size of the Giver.

A decade ago, I wrestled with the deepest despair of my life, wondering why God would have left me on this earth after my stroke. I was broken in body, brain, and spirit, unable to do anything or be anything other than a source of pain for everyone I loved. It seemed that everyone would eventually stop being so sad if I weren't here anymore. God had obviously made a mistake. But over time, I was able to hear God's words in my heart: "You are not a mistake because I don't make mistakes. There is purpose—just wait, you'll see."

If we have a pulse, we have a purpose. We are not still on earth by accident. We are here today because we've been called by God to this unique place and circumstance, to this moment in time and history. We're here because there's more life for us to experience and more work for us to do and more love for us to give. If we can't fathom why or figure out how, it doesn't matter; we don't have to know all those answers before we start living. In fact, those questions can't begin to be answered until we step into this new normal life first. We are all living out some version of a second chance; some of us are just more aware of it than others. Our second-chance life is not the one just out of reach; it's the one right in front of us. It's the one God has been calling us to all along.

The Ultimate Calling

The prophet Isaiah described a voice calling to "prepare the way for the LORD" in the wilderness (Isaiah 40:3). And he depicted a stunning picture of this preparation as the world leveling out—the mountains being made low and the valleys being lifted up to make a straight path for God. There are no more obstacles. There are no more hierarchies. God can come, and His glory can be seen by everyone. As God calls us onto the straight paths He has laid out for us, it seems He is also calling us to make a straight path for Him.

John the Baptist quoted the same verse from Isaiah when asked if he was in fact the Messiah. "No, I'm just preparing the way for Him and calling anyone else who will listen to do the same" (John 1:23, my paraphrase). John was the forerunner to Jesus. He went ahead of Him and made a way for Him to come. And Jesus is our forerunner, as we see in Hebrews 6:19–20, which just so happens to be the inspiration passage for our ministry: "We have this hope as an anchor for the soul, firm and secure. It enters the inner sanctuary behind the curtain, where our forerunner, Jesus, has entered on our behalf."

This is admittedly a weird picture, but I can't help but think of an "upside-down kingdom" anchor when I think of this passage. The anchor is an ancient symbol of hope, helping save a ship from being destroyed by the storms. And Jesus as our anchor takes this hope to a deeper level. He doesn't just save us from the storms but helps us rise above them. If you look at an anchor, you'll see the shape of a cross in it, so it just makes too much sense, right? I picture our Jesus anchor as not sinking beneath the water but rising above it into the sky, breaking through clouds and unseen dimensions and returning to God. And like all anchors, this one has a chain, and it dangles down to us, offering a connection to hope and a path to God.

Here's where it gets wild. John was Jesus' forerunner. Jesus is our forerunner. And now it seems we've been called to be Jesus' forerunner, to go ahead of Him and make a way for Him to come again. We are called to prepare a way for the Lord. Yet often we feel unworthy and ill-equipped. Certainly the task of leveling mountains and raising valleys seems beyond our understanding and pay grade. But looking back a few verses earlier in John 1, we see an explanation of how John the Baptist prepared the way for Jesus and how we might prepare the way too. It simply says that John prepared the way when he became a witness who testified about the light (John 1:7).

I've watched my fair share of police procedurals and court-room dramas on TV. Since Jay even went to law school, we know some courtroom basics. The conflict is between the main play-ers—a defendant and a plaintiff—who are advocated for by their lawyers. Then the judge and jury decide the outcome. There's also a court reporter who takes notes and a bailiff who makes sassy commentary to the judge. Oh, and there are also witnesses who testify about their experience. And according to John, we are called to that role—to be witnesses.

Typically, we think of ourselves as the main players; we're the wronged or the accused who must fight our way through. If not that, then we're the ones fighting for others, making our case for justice. And if not that, then at least we get to be the decision maker who hears the arguments and offers our great wisdom to determine truth and outcomes. But here in this earth-shattering calling to prepare the way of the Lord, to level out the earth, to make a straight and smooth path for God so His glory can be seen by everyone, we are simply called to be *witnesses*. What? Witnesses don't even get to make closing statements! Witnesses may seem like the most D-level stars in this drama, but maybe that's the point. It's not all about us. In fact, this never was our case to win or lose. That's God's job.

And it's pretty cool to think that God is actually playing all the roles in this cosmic courtroom. He is the judge and jury. Jesus is the defendant and the plaintiff. The Holy Spirit is the advocate. Maybe angels are the bailiff and court reporter. You get the point. But we are still invited into the room. We are not the light, but we testify about the light. Despite this seemingly insignificant role, a witness can play a vital role in the outcome of the case. A witness's experience can change everything. Yet all a witness is called to do is tell his or her own true story. All we are called to do is tell ours.

Our story begins with first paying attention to God's story. We don't have to fight so hard. We don't have to judge so hard. All we have to do is remember the story of our life with God and tell about it. And as the words come out of our mouths, the mountains of privilege and self-actualization, the valleys of brokenness and despair, rumble to a level ground. In that place, God's glory can be seen by everyone.

Hope It Forward

During these years when we lost so much and yet were filled up with even more, the question became, *What are we supposed to do now?* We're new people on the other side of this suffering.

We've been given a second chance. We've been left with a story that has changed us and other people too. We didn't know where we would be years down the road, but we knew we'd been called to take what we'd been given and give it away. God never calls us to give from a void, but rather He calls us to give from what He has already given us.

Paul described this in 2 Corinthians 1:3–5: "Praise be to . . . the God of all comfort, who comforts us in all our troubles, so that we can comfort those in any trouble with the comfort we ourselves receive from God. For just as we share abundantly in the sufferings of Christ, so also our comfort abounds through Christ." For a God who wastes nothing and withholds no good thing, it's fitting that He creates a perpetual circuit of hope and comfort through us as living conduits. He gives us what we give away, but in the giving away, we are quite miraculously, but not surprisingly, filled back up.

Romans 15:13 proclaims, "May the God of hope fill you with all joy and peace as you trust in him, so that you may overflow with hope by the power of the Holy Spirit." We are filled with hope so that we can be overwhelmed by and overflow with it. We like to call this "hoping it forward," and this calling continues to be a motivating charge to get out of bed every morning into an unknown future and a life we never saw ourselves living.

As nice as it sounds to "hope it forward," it actually runs counter to the culture and to the visceral callings we hear in the midst of our pain. When we've been through suffering, we think the end goal of us being comforted is so we can be comfortable. We think we are the beginning and end of our suffering and our comfort. And we certainly don't like the idea of taking something valuable that we've been given and giving it away. Yet in this process of refining us, God cautions that we'll never triumph over our pain if we keep the comfort all to ourselves. Our suffering is bigger than ourselves, but our healing is bigger than ourselves too.

This is why community is absolutely necessary in the redefining of our calling. We'll never know the biggest vision God has for our lives and this world until we see that vision reflected in someone else's story. We'll never gain a true perspective on all we've been given and all we'll never be able to do by ourselves until we open our deepest hopes and fears to each other.

When we began hearing the stories of struggle and loss, the stories of flourishing through suffering, the stories of families with disabilities like us for whom the world wasn't made, our calling became clearer. We'd been lifted up by deep relationships, renewed by necessary rest, and empowered by life-giving resources. For some reason, we'd been given these things, and they had helped heal us and empower us. Why couldn't we help give those same things away to families like us? So we did. Hope Heals Camp became the vehicle to "hope it forward" and to encourage the campers to do the same when they got home.

That prompted the question, *How can we end each day of camp on the right note?* Our little family of four has a nightly ritual we've kept for many years. It signals to our bodies and brains that the day is ending and night is coming. We click off the lights and sit at the edge of our kids' beds in the dark. And we sing a blessing from Numbers 6 to the tune of "Edelweiss." Now, bedtime at our house rarely looks like the choreographed lovefest of children in matching outfits singing in harmony toward the end of *The Sound of Music*, though it sometimes looks more like the scenes at the beginning when they would torture the nanny who would later teach them to sing and be their new mom. But we sing it to them because God has sung it to us. "May the Lord, mighty God, bless and keep you forever; grant you peace, perfect peace, courage in every endeavor. Lift up your eyes and see His face, know His grace is for you; may the Lord, mighty God, bless and keep you forever." And sometimes our tired hearts sing it in double time, and sometimes it's just a duet we parents sing over our sleeping or disinterested kids, but on rare occasions, all four of us spontaneously sing the words to each other, for each other, from God and to Him, in the dark, and it's magical.

We decided there was no better way to end each night of camp than by gathering in a giant circle where we hold hands and sing that same blessing based on Numbers 6. The song has echoed over my life longer than I can remember. It has been sung back to me by others who now sing it and remember who God has called them to be too. And it will continue reverberating in my soul until I can't even remember anymore. It's a calling to God's peace and His courage. It's a calling to look up to His grace. It's the universal calling for all of us, and at the same time it's a personal revelation that says, "Who else could this have happened to but you?"

CHAPTER 12

WAITING WELL

Redefining Hope

Jay

It was a Sunday morning when she fainted. Amid the pre-church commotion of second cups of coffee and still-not-yet-dressed children, Katherine stood up from the couch and then promptly fell over like a tree. Her long legs didn't even bend. Her body didn't even crumple. She fell over in a straight line, rather miraculously missing the sharp edges of nearby furniture and toys. I yelled in a decidedly non–Sunday morning kind of way and rushed to her to assess the damage. Sadly, it wasn't my first time at this rodeo, or hers either, and I breathlessly checked for major injuries, but unlike past falls due to her impaired balance, this time she had clearly passed out. She came to confusedly, not sure how she had ended up on the floor. We both realized as her body yelled "Timber!" that she had sloshed the last of her cup of coffee onto our then two-year-old, John, but thankfully the coffee was cold.

He was her first concern. We quickly pivoted from church preparations and prepared to head to the ER.

Thankfully, we hadn't spent much time in the hospital in that season compared to the near-constant visits in the years following Katherine's stroke as she underwent eleven surgeries and had ongoing therapy and follow-up appointments. The one benefit of having spent lots of time in the hospital is that you at least know the drill, and if you're lucky, you know some people who can help you. The not-so-beneficial part of having spent lots of time in the hospital is that you are acutely aware that an ordinary day can turn into a life-changing one. Anything can happen. We texted Katherine's neurosurgeon, Dr. Nestor Gonzalez, on our way to the ER. Not only had he performed the surgery that saved her life in 2008, but he had removed a totally unrelated brain aneurysm in 2013, which paved the way for her to get pregnant with John *Nestor* Wolf. (It seems only fitting to name your miracle child after your miracle-working doctor.)

Katherine had been getting annual brain scans to check up on what is clearly an impaired neurovascular system. A few months prior, she had gotten a scan, along with a big thumbs-up from Dr. Gonzalez. This was both comforting and disconcerting. Surely nothing has changed since then and she's fine. Maybe it's just a blood sugar thing? But then the other voice in my head spoke, the one that says, "But bad things have happened in the past, and that means they can happen again."

I manage stress pretty well. I wish my go-to stress relievers were running until the sun goes down and having no appetite; I'm kind of the opposite of those, but I guess you can't have it all.

As we waited for the MRI, I desperately tried to hide my concern from Katherine—from behind a piece of pizza, no less—so as to not stress her out. I rubbed her feet and tried to distract her with pics of our kids and funny videos on my phone. She manages stress pretty well too, but as a human being and nonrobot, she maintains some very real responses to fear and the unknown, and oftentimes, her responses are linked to mine.

Unfortunately, she had developed a growing claustrophobia in the MRI machine. She does not deal with anxiety much, but understandably having your head locked down onto a bed with half your body in a tube and half hanging out is not a very peaceful situation. And a few years ago, a rather thoughtless technician had left her strapped inside the machine and walked off for a few minutes while leaving the door to the room open. *Hi, everyone. I'm just here in my hospital gown, thinking all the bad thoughts, exposed in all the worst ways.*

Moreover, these kinds of scans can tee up another kind of unique experience—the pit-in-your-stomach kind of fear in the waiting for an answer in the unknown. I had kind of forgotten that my life wasn't normal, but now I was reminded and needed to know, *Is there another problem? Is my life going to change again before I leave this place?* Just a few existential moments to ponder on an ordinary morning with your doctor. I would normally drop her off and wait outside during every other similar scan, but today, it seemed we both needed to be physical reminders for each other that we were not alone.

Stress may not inspire physical running for me, but it definitely inspires laps and laps of mental miles to be run. The medical advocate in me wasn't taking no for an answer, and I finagled and persuaded my way into the actual MRI room with her, positioning my chair at just the right angle so we could see each other and just close enough so I could give her leg a reassuring squeeze. Clearly, the full hour's-worth of scans ordered by Dr. Gonzalez signaled he was concerned too. Knowing her brain was seemingly in good shape based on the scans from a few months before, he wanted to investigate every nook and cranny.

After an initial review of the scans, the on-call ER doctor told us everything actually looked okay, and we should go home. Whew! That was a close one. He didn't have to tell us twice. We left feeling grateful to have escaped from the hospital once again. We were tired but relatively unscathed. And though we still didn't know the cause of the fainting, we prayed it was just a one-off thing we had been overly cautious about.

The next morning, we got the call. "Please come back to the hospital immediately. We found something." Apparently, things hadn't sat quite right with Dr. Gonzalez, and he did a deeper dive into all the scans. Katherine's brain was in fact working well. There was no reason for her to not be getting enough oxygen and thus pass out—until Dr. Gonzalez looked outside of her brain to the vertebral artery in the back of her neck, one of the major sources of blood to the brain, and found the issue. There was a tear in that artery that was causing a blood clot to form and was literally blocking the blood flow to her brain. She was essentially on the verge of having another major stroke for a totally different reason than the one before.

VADs (vertebral artery dissections) are more common in women and are the result of major or minor trauma from things like repeatedly holding the phone to your ear with your neck, getting your hair washed in a salon on top of those uncomfortable bowls, the awkward falling-asleep neck snap when you nod off on an airplane, or an inexperienced chiropractic adjustment. Yep, it's officially confirmed: the world is not a safe place when a trip to the hair salon or a phone chat could end in death. And even more frustrating, Katherine had not had any of those experiences! Though she'd been experiencing some neck and shoulder pain, she had lumped it in with her chronic back pain.

We would actually never learn a root cause of her VAD and thus a way to prevent future VADs. The most likely culprit is the general and ongoing trauma of having a body that doesn't totally work right, along with deafness and double vision that require her to turn her head around often to figure out what's going on in the world—oh, and crazy people (or children) who come up behind her, tapping her shoulder or bear-hugging her with unexpected and unwanted force.

That ordinary Sunday morning morphed into a four-day hospital stay with a blood thinner regimen before she was finally cleared to go back into the unsafe and unknown world to heal. Her own blood would be the way her body would heal itself over time, but the effects of the blood thinner, Coumadin—a medicine originally invented for use as rat poison—would be intense. There would be increased dizziness and nausea, not to mention the constant fear of falling while on a blood thinner, which Katherine was prone to do anyway. It was an anxiety-inducing season to say the least, and you'd better believe that when she was cleared to get off that nasty stuff six months later, we all did a happy dance.

Those few days in the hospital were a kind of unexpected reflection on all the lessons we'd learned together staring at hospital room ceilings for the past decade. We realized that everything we'd discovered through our struggles was still true. The story we had told ourselves all these years about who God was and what He was doing in our pain had not taken away our future struggles, but it had taken away some of the overwhelming fear, sadness, and doubts. In their place, we had a new peace and a deep trust that we were going to be okay, no matter what happened, because it was all still true.

Yet that experience and all the ones before it and all the ones to come after it remind us that our future in this world will always be outside our control. It will always be *unknown*. Katherine may go through all these bodily struggles and still live to be 110. Maybe I will too, though that sounds pretty old to be still hanging out here. Maybe our health and our family and our finances and our minds and our memories will be strong and good. Or maybe they won't. Today could be the best day, the worst day, or the last day of our lives. But we don't have to live in fear. Even in the face of the unknown, we can remember what and who we do know, and help each other remember it too. In so doing, we can start to know the truest things again. We can preach them to our own hearts until we actually believe them.

Bargaining with God

Knowing that much of life is out of our control should actually be a call to action. We may be powerless in some ways, but we're not helpless. We can still pursue our dreams without clasping them to our chests, and bucket lists can be a helpful way to be intentional with our lives before we "kick the bucket."

However, we can get pretty mixed-up on this bucket list thing. After the stroke, we threw our bucket list and lots of other future plans out the window. We figured the real bucket list was just still being here and not actually kicking the bucket yet! As life moved forward, we became a little more confident that there were some dreams we did want to keep, and we wanted to pat ourselves on the back for things we had never thought to put on the list but could now check off. We traced our finger down to the line item for SUFFERING. Check. Woo-hoo! Now we could move on to the skydiving and tropical vacation . . . or maybe just the tropical vacation. And just think how much more we'd appreciate it now because of all the hard stuff we'd made it through. *It's a deal, God! Thank You!* I'm not sure God rolled His eyes at us—it might be beneath Him—but He also just might have.

Sometimes our attempts to make deals with God are explicit and well-thought-out on our end, but more often, they're subtle and sometimes even unconscious. We bargain: "God, since we've already been through so much, it stands to reason that we shouldn't have to go through more hard stuff. You know, the balancing-rules-of-the-universe thing." Or "God, I get how You have used my pain. I'm processing that still, and ya know, I think I'm good. I don't need any more 'helpful' experiences like this in my future, but thanks." Or the classic, "I promise to be so good from here on out. I'll dedicate my life to You. I'll go to church and not get on Instagram so much and actually put money in the offering plate.

You have my word." Or we get a little feisty: "God, no more! Done and done. This isn't fair. This isn't the life You promised! I already checked *Suffering* off the bucket list too!" We effectively unroll our contract and shove it in God's face. But soon enough we realize that a contract requires two signatures, and this one only has ours on it. And we also realize we've written it in crayon, with the cute backward *R*s. I think if there was an eye roll from God before, now there's more of a loving sigh.

God, who is the most brilliant negotiator, the fairest judge, and the most tireless advocate, is not ruffled by our demands. Rather, He looks us straight in the eyes, face-to-face, firm hands on our shoulders, soft smile reverberating into our souls, and asks us a question: "What is it you want from Me?" We might be taken aback by the question. We might have a harsh and definitive answer, a rebuttal, hard facts, persuasion. Instead, we realize we're standing at a crossroads with Him.

"What is it you want from Me? Do you want Me to give you the gifts and the life you think you're entitled to? Or do you want to know the Giver of every good and perfect gift? Do you just want to stop hurting? Or do you want to know the Healer of the world? I'm offering you everything. I'm offering you Me." Is God what we want—to know Him and make Him known, to love Him and be loved by Him? Or do we think He's just really good at giving us all the things we don't have?

This is the question we must grapple with every day as we wake up to the unknown. In the words of the indomitable Corrie ten Boom, "Never be afraid to trust an unknown future to a known God."[25] But it's only fair to acknowledge that God can often seem far more unknowable than an unknown tomorrow. And of course, this makes it harder to want Him over wanting things we can wrap our heads around more easily. It's easier to want our bodies to work right or the relationship to stay strong or the pain to go away than it is to say, "But Your will be done . . . whatever that will may be." And yet knowing God and wanting Him are inextricably linked. When we choose to open our hearts and receive Him on His terms, we really begin to know Him. And when we begin to know Him, we more readily open our hearts to receive more of Him. This cycle of building trust becomes a holy unraveling of ourselves and a stunning revelation of Him.

There is simply no shortcut to knowing God. It's not a simple one, two, three steps. Rather, it's a journey of asking, seeking, and knocking—and then finding. Then doing it all over again in different ways and in different seasons. It's about finding all of God's spectacular attributes in Jesus—"the image of the invisible God" (Colossians 1:15). It's about finding God's grandeur in the natural world and universe. It's about finding God's heartbreak and love for us in other human beings. It's about finding God Himself as we talk to Him and listen for Him in prayer and meditation. It's about asking His Holy Spirit to connect all the pieces until we have a picture of His awe-inspiring magnificence. Even then, we may not always like or fully understand what we find, because in the hard search for God, we find out hard things about ourselves.

When Job lamented his horrifying plight and cried out to God, God made no apologies for the reality that He is God and Job was not. In fact, He kind of went for it in hammering home the point for several chapters. He reminded Job that, though He loved Job with an everlasting love, Job was not His equal. Not even close. They weren't even in the same universe or same dimension. There was no bargain. There was no partnership. And yet God still wanted Job. When Job finally got this, he saw who he was dealing with. Job didn't have any more words; he just had awe.

Talk about a new perspective! Job had heard of God, but now he had seen Him. And this happens for any of us who are willing to offer ourselves up to God in this vulnerable posture. It happened for Corrie ten Boom in the concentration camps of Nazi Germany, and she found a way to trust God in the midst of huge losses and huge fears. It has happened for countless sinners and saints over the course of human history. It has happened for us.

In the end, Job received restoration, even an increase, of much of what had been lost. It's tempting to think that if we just pray the prayer, if we just acknowledge God like Job did, then God will give us back what we don't have. And He may even double our finances! But when we read more closely, we see that God gave Job more children but didn't bring back the ones he'd lost. He restored his fortunes but didn't return what almost anyone would consider to be his greatest treasure. Did Job not pray quite right? Did he lack faith? Was he being punished? Didn't he and God have a deal? But then we realize there's no shortcut. There's no way to fully wrap our heads around God. He is good, but can we fathom what the depth of goodness in Him really means? He is holy. He is other. He is God. We are not, and that's actually a very, very good thing.

Waiting in the Dark

One of God's greatest gifts to me in seasons of both stress and calm has been my ability to sleep like the dead. I sometimes realize I'm snoring before I even knew I was asleep! I consider it a nice consolation prize for living a rather tiring life, and yet I know that sleep often eludes even the weariest of souls. This includes my lovely wife. She is not plagued with insomnia or restless leg syndrome, thankfully, but perhaps even worse, or at least more puzzlingly, she has suffered from night terrors since childhood. To her parents' horror, they would hear someone bumping around in their house at night, only to find to their continued horror that it was young Katherine trying to unlock the front door and wander around outside at 3:00 a.m. And sadly, marriage did not cure what ails her. I finally had to learn to not have a heart attack at 3:00 a.m. when Katherine breathlessly told me in the same creepy cadence as "I see dead people" that she was in fact seeing very real people in our totally empty, dark bedroom. We could have perhaps had a very bizarre and successful reality show exploiting this regular nighttime craziness.

Surely there is some logical psychoanalysis to be done. Some connection to her mind/body/soul or the space-time continuum. We've had a sleep study on our medical to-do list for a while, but it keeps getting pushed down the list. Regardless of the root cause, this condition keeps bedtime interesting. Once we lie down, we never know what we're going to get!

And I also find it more entertaining to speculate with my own cobbled-together science that her night terrors are a by-product of a very duck-like brain. We've all got the animalistic parts of our brain that come out at inopportune times. Apparently, birds and other aquatic mammals sleep with one-half of their brains fully resting while the other half remains fully awake. This no doubt helps prevent all kinds of cute sleeping animals from falling off logs into water, and I suppose it also helps them not to get eaten by predators. I would absolutely sleep with one eye open if I had to sleep on a log or in the ocean.

Totally makes sense. At night, Katherine's brain isn't necessarily fearing predators, but more broadly an unsafe world that feels even more unknowable every time the sun sets. Particularly since becoming disabled, Katherine's night terrors have sadly increased. No doubt it's because the darkness of sleep signals the possibility of unknown threats from which she would have a hard time running away. The darkness doesn't feel safe, and it isn't.

And yet even those of us who can run away more easily still find ourselves with a sense of dread when we can't fully see what's ahead or behind us. Sometimes there is nothing else to do but wait with our fears in the dark, covers pulled up around our heads, until the literal or figurative sun comes up and we can see more clearly again. It's hardwired in our brains and in our experiences and in our spiritual lives too. Darkness has never had a very redemptive ring to it. The forces of darkness don't seem to be a team we'd want to play on. And yet as with most things we're afraid of, there may be more to learn in the dark than in the light.

A family in our church tragically lost their college-aged daughter in a car accident. Their lives were suddenly plunged into a unique kind of darkness, as if stepping into an unforeseen hole and free-falling down deep into blackness. They had known God before, and they found Him again there with them. They had come across Isaiah 45:3 and had clung to it and to God as they waited for light to invade their blackest night: "I will give you hidden treasures, riches stored in secret places, so that you may know that I am the Lord, the God of Israel, who summons you by name." In that dark place of shocking grief, in the waiting and not knowing, they determined to not waste their stay. As Katherine has so poignantly said, "If I have to go into the darkness, you'd better believe I'm going to get some treasure out of it!"

Barbara Brown Taylor writes, "New life starts in the dark. Whether it is a seed in the ground, a baby in the womb, or Jesus in the tomb, it starts in the dark."[26] And it does. As much as we don't imagine it that way and pray for anything but, there is new life and treasure and God there. We can trust Him to share His gifts in the dark. And because of this, we have a boundless hope.

In Romans 5, Paul paints an otherworldly picture of metamorphosis that takes us from deepest suffering to boundless hope. Paul is saying that we can wait well during our deepest pains; we can persevere because we know our suffering will not be in vain. We can wait well for anything, as long as we know we will eventually get even more than what we've been waiting for. In fact, what we get at the end of our waiting will be so good that it will make us *glory* in our sufferings because of what the process has birthed in us.

When suffering turns off the distractions of the ordinary and highlights the peace and grace coursing through us, it can also highlight our character in a way never before realized. There is no hiding when we are forced to wait. Our deepest vulnerabilities, struggles, temptations, and flaws are laid bare, if to no one else but us. There is nothing to cover up the things we see in the mirror. There is no screen or instant outcome or busywork to distract us when everything else falls away. Our character is revealed, and maybe for the first time, in the space of our waiting, we get to be real with ourselves. *What motivates me? What scares me? What do I really want?* In asking these questions, we slowly find the answers. If we get answers we don't want or don't like, we get to begin the process of change while we continue to wait.

Joan Didion explains character as "the willingness to accept responsibility for one's own life."[27] This life and this waiting are our own, and they're ours to own. In the waiting, self-actualization, distraction, and unwillingness to take up the cause of the oppressed are all called to task. These things are not character. This is not the way to hope. Yet the character formed in the waiting is not moral perfection. Far from it. In fact, we are confronted with just how far from perfect we are. True character is about acknowledging just how hard it is to be what we know we can be and then still seeking to become it.

When we wait in faith and trust, we are met with grace and peace. It's not our own efforts that sustain us, but the efforts of Jesus—the work that is already complete—that embolden us and empower us to wait well. Ironically, more acute suffering can spur a more acute awareness of the peace we receive in our waiting, and thus a greater dependence on it to persevere. The peace is there, buzzing through us, whether or not we notice, but sometimes suffering knocks out the other competing systems long enough for us to finally realize what that peculiar noise was all along. We find that the otherwise loathed and laborious process of becoming is something we never would have avoided had we known what we'd find at the end of the day—the hope we need the most.

Unlike other finite outcomes, hope is a future promise lived out in the present. In its truest and most potent form, it cannot be conjured or willed into existence. It's not dependent on our ability to feel it or keep it going. It, like the grace and peace coursing through us, has been there all along. Betting our lives and our hurts, our waiting and our future, on this kind of hope will never put us to shame. This is because hope is not simply a feeling projected in our own image, wrought with our imperfections and inconsistencies; rather, it is a limitless well. It is the water of life that will never run dry. It is life and light. Hope for an unknown future has always been found in a known God . . . Jesus. And He is worth waiting for.

A New Name

Some dear friends in Los Angeles would throw an annual Christmas event for a group of kids living in the foster system. LA's foster system, like most foster systems, is horrifically under-resourced and overwhelmed. Talk about feeling unworthy—many of these kids have bounced from foster home to group home and back again a dozen times in their short years of life. The unspoken question *Why doesn't anybody want me?* emanates from the crowd as they enter the space decked out with every imaginable

Christmas decoration and treat. Then their eyes widen, tentatively at first, and just a little. *Is someone actually seeing me? Wanting to know me? Offering to help me? Wanting nothing in return?*

A breakfast buffet extends along one wall of the room, and a pile of presents for each child lines the other wall. Blankets and beanbags are scattered around for each child to sit on as if they were in their own living room surrounded by a family that loves them—and in a way, they are. Our friend JT, one of the most gregarious people we know, offers a greeting to these new friends as they are each handed a name tag. It takes a moment to process that everyone is given one without even being asked their name. They all look down to read the words they wear on their chests. The smiles start to spread, and so do the tears, as JT tells them that no matter what names they came into that place with, they also got a new name today: "Chosen." "Mine." "Empowered." "Family." "Beautiful." "Known." "Beloved."

It's not so different when we venture toward God. We don't know what to expect. We have been defined by our identity, our fears, our wounds, our longings. But then the confetti starts to drop, and in His best Oprah-esque giveaway voice, arms spread wide, He booms, "You get a new name! And *you* get a new name!" He puts new name tags over our hearts, covering the ones we've worn for as long as we can remember. This love of God is a force that heals every broken place and changes every seemingly unchangeable thing. No, we won't walk away from love unscathed. It will change us, if we let it.

Yes, life defines us. But suffering strong can redefine us. Ultimately, perfect love refines us as it reminds us that God calls us by name and sings over us in our darkness. He sings a song of blessing. A song of promise. A song of hope. Jesus, the wounded Healer, invites us to take the same journey He did, the only one that ends in transformation and new life. We know the end of the story of suffering in the world. We know it is overcome by a hope that will never die.

Friend, even if you must blindly walk through the valley of the shadow of death, be assured that you're only walking in a shadow, not in death itself. You're surrounded by night, but it's surrounded by light. Listen for your name. It will sound like a mom calling her son to come in at twilight just in time for supper, or a dad waking his daughter from a deep sleep with the sure sound of his voice. It may still be dark, but it will feel like home.

THE GOOD/HARD LIFE

Katherine

We tucked our kids in bed at the end of the long day. They protested. We protested right back. It was time. We prayed and sang in our usual way, but for some reason that night, I was prompted to offer one last seed to the soil of their nearly sleeping heads and hearts. Maybe it was a response to their time-honored request for God to help them just "have a good day tomorrow" or their subtly communicated fear of the future and not-so-subtle fear of the dark. It seemed another truer word needed to be spoken aloud.

As we knelt by their silhouettes, this tearful declaration sprang from my lips with surprising strength and clarity, perhaps because I had been telling it to my own heart all along: "James and John, God made you to do the hard thing in the good story He's writing for your life. Whether tomorrow is the best or worst or last day of our lives, we pray that God will give us everything we need to live it out to the fullest with courage and joy."

This is the good/hard life. This is the way of Jesus. The way of glory through sacrifice, flourishing within limitations. And with unstoppable love coursing through the whole thing, it is golden. It will be hard, but we have already been made for the hard. God has equipped us with everything we need for the journey ahead, most of all with Himself. And the story being written—unexpected and painful and long or short as it may be—will still be good because He can't write any other kind of story.

Life is never just one note. It's too dynamic for that. And how much more so God. Don't settle for a whistle when there's a symphony surrounding you. Don't believe the lie that it must be one or the other, because you'll be missing out on something vital—the experience of life's true fullness. Good and hard are not mutually exclusive. This side of heaven they are equal halves of a bittersweet whole. They reveal each other. The more the hard carves out tender places in your heart, the more space there is for the good to fill it in. And the more good fills up in your life, the more overflow there will be onto the hard work ahead. This is the way where new beginnings come out of what looks like the ending.

I pray my boys never stop believing that good things will come to their lives, but I also pray for a redefining of just what good means to them in this upside-down kingdom of God. And if the day or their lives don't look anything like they thought, I pray God will empower them with bravery to illuminate the darkness and help them uncover every last bit of treasure to be found there.

This message is the message of my life and of every life awakened to its own broken-down but miraculous nature. It has taken time and tears, along with many teachers and much grace, to uncover it, and even more of all those things to actually believe it. But now, my upended life has revealed my second-chance life. The redefining of me has become the refined me. And I truly love my life. I want to cherish it and champion it, even the parts I never could have imagined. And I want to live it well to the very end. May it be so for us all.

ACKNOWLEDGMENTS

The message of this book has been welling up in us for years, but an entire village helped bring it out . . .

To our boys, James and John, thank you for living this good/hard life to the fullest with us.

To our families, thank you for encouraging us to lean into this unique message and calling on our lives.

To our Hope Heals Camp community, thank you for making the invisible God and His upside-down kingdom visible to us. We will never be the same after knowing you.

To our M.O.R.E. ladies, thank you for creating a safe space to wrestle through this journey of redefining. The message of this book is a direct overflow from the years of our pajama-clad early mornings together in Culver City.

To our Seasons Weekend family, thank you for calling out things in us we didn't yet see in ourselves and for making a place for us not only to see those things more clearly but to share them too.

To Joni and Friends, thank you for paving the way for another miracle girl in a wheelchair to tell people about Jesus.

To our LA small group, thank you for teaching us the deep and hard-won lessons of true community and life together.

To our Bel Air Church community, thank you for helping us find a home before everything changed and a voice after everything changed.

To our Passion City Church community, thank you for offering deep healing to our hearts long before we would actually call you friends. You have fanned into flame the spark of our hope like none other.

To our Hope Heals team and supporters, thank you for joining us on this wild ride. You are the glue that holds us together and the coffee that keeps us moving forward.

To our Zondervan Books team, thank you for guiding us through this uphill process and for helping take this vital message to people and places we would never be able to reach on our own.

NOTES

1. Our thoughts about the theme of flourishing within the limitations of disability were influenced by a talk we heard by Kate Harris about thriving within the context of motherhood ("Motherhood as Vocation," Washington Institute for Faith, Vocation and Culture, https://washingtoninst.org/motherhood-as-vocation).

2. Flannery O'Connor, *Mystery and Manners: Occasional Prose* (New York: Farrar, Straus, and Giroux, 1963), 171.

3. Dorothy Sayers, *Letters to a Diminished Church: Passionate Arguments for the Relevance of Christian Doctrine* (Nashville: W Publishing, 2004), 2.

4. Dietrich Bonhoeffer, *Letters and Papers from Prison* (1953; repr., New York: Touchstone, 1997), 176.

5. Quoted in Alina Tugend, "Colleges Grapple with Where—or Whether—to Draw the Line on Free Speech," *New York Times*, June 5, 2018, www.nytimes.com/2018/06/05/education/learning /colleges-free-speech.html.

6. Cited in Jane McGonigal, "The Game That Can Give You 10 Extra Years of Life," TED Global 2012, www.ted.com/talks/jane _mcgonigal_the_game_that_can_give_you_10_extra_years_of_life.

7. Used by permission.

8. Sir Richard Baker, *Meditations and Disquisitions upon the First Psalm, the Penitential Psalms, and Seven Consolatory Psalms* (London: Higham, 1882), 392.

9. Oliver Sacks, "My Own Life," *New York Times*, February 19, 2015, www.nytimes.com/2015/02/19/opinion/oliver-sacks-on-learning-he -has-terminal-cancer.html.

10. Atul Gawande, *Being Mortal: Medicine and What Matters in the End* (New York: Metropolitan Books, 2014).

11. Mike Foster, Rescue Academy LIVE workshop, www.rescueacademy .com.

12. Rick Warren, *The Purpose Driven® Life: What on Earth Am I Here For?* (2002; repr., Grand Rapids: Zondervan, 2012), 149.

13. Fyodor Dostoevsky, *The Idiot: A Novel in Four Parts* (New York: Macmillan, 1915), 383.

14. Elisabeth Kübler-Ross, *Death: The Final Stage of Growth* (New York: Touchstone, 1975), 96.

15. Cited in Christopher Perrin, PhD, "Loving What Must Be Done," Inside Classical Education, July 31, 2012, https://insideclassicaled.com /2012/07.

16. See C. S. Lewis, *Mere Christianity* (1952; repr., New York: HarperCollins, 2001), 131–32.

17. Bonhoeffer, *Letters and Papers from Prison*, 43.

18. Brené Brown, *The Gifts of Imperfection: Let Go of Who You Think You're Supposed to Be and Embrace Who You Are* (Center City, MN: Hazelden, 2010), 26.

19. Mary Oliver, "Sometimes," in *Redbird: Poems by Mary Oliver* (Boston: Beacon, 2009), 37.

20. See James W. Pennebaker, *The Secret Life of Pronouns: What Our Words Say about Us* (New York: Bloomsbury, 2011).

21. Pennebaker, *Secret Life of Pronouns*, 109–10.

22. Wendell Berry, "Marriage," in *The Selected Poems of Wendell Berry* (Berkeley, CA: Counterpoint, 1998), 31.

23. Martin Luther King Jr., *Strength to Love* (New York: Harper & Row, 1963), 37.

24. Katherine and Jay Wolf, *Hope Heals: A True Story of Overwhelming Loss and an Overcoming Love* (Grand Rapids: Zondervan, 2016), 236.

25. Corrie ten Boom, *Each New Day: 365 Simple Reflections* (1977; repr., Grand Rapids: Revell, 2003), 73.

26. Barbara Brown Taylor, *Learning to Walk in the Dark* (New York: HarperOne, 2014), 129.

27. Joan Didion, "On Self-Respect: Joan Didion's 1961 Essay from the Pages of *Vogue*," *Vogue*, October 22, 2014, www.vogue.com/article /joan-didion-self-respect-essay-1961.

Hope Heals

A True Story of Overwhelming Loss and an Overcoming Love

Katherine and Jay Wolf

*When all seems lost,
where can hope be found?*

Katherine and Jay married right after college and sought adventure far from home in Los Angeles. As they pursued their dreams—she as a model and he as a lawyer—they planted their lives in the city and in their church community. Their son, James, came along unexpectedly in the fall of 2007, and just six months later, everything changed in a moment for this young family.

On April 21, 2008, as James slept in the other room, Katherine collapsed, suffering a massive brain stem stroke without warning. Miraculously, Jay came home in time and called for help. Katherine was immediately rushed into micro-brain surgery, though her chance of survival was slim. As the sun rose the next morning, the surgeon proclaimed that Katherine had survived the removal of part of her brain, though her future recovery was completely uncertain. Yet in that moment, there was a spark of hope. Through forty days on life support in the ICU and nearly two years in full-time brain rehab, that spark of hope was fanned into flame.

Defying every prognosis with grit and grace, Katherine and Jay, side by side, struggled to regain a life for Katherine as she relearned to talk and eat and walk. Returning home with a severely disabled body but a completely renewed purpose, they committed to celebrate this gift of a second chance by embracing life fully, even though that life looked very different than they could have ever imagined. In the midst of continuing hardships and struggles, both in body and mind, Katherine and Jay found what we all long to find... hope—hope that heals the most broken place, our souls.

An excruciating yet beautiful road to recovery has led the Wolf family to their new normal, in which almost every moment of life is marked with the scars of that fateful April day in 2008. Now, many years later, Katherine and Jay are stewarding their story of suffering, restoration, and Christ-centered hope in this broken world through their ministry Hope Heals.

Available in stores and online!